The Art
OF SELLING YOUR
BANK

A Bank CEO's Step-By-Step Guide

KURT KNUTSON

DISCLAIMER

While intended to be accurate and authoritative information regarding the matter covered, the information provided in this book is for informational purposes only and is not intended to be a source of advice or analysis. The information and/or documents contained in this book are not banking, legal, or financial advice and should never be used without first consulting with a professional to determine what may be best for your individual needs. No warranty may be created or extended by sales representatives or written sales materials.

The author and publisher make no warranty, guarantee, or other promise as to any results that may be obtained from utilizing this book. The advice and strategies contained in this book may not be suitable for your position. Prior to any financial decision, you should first consult with your financial advisor and conduct due diligence and research. To the maximum extent permitted by law, the author and publisher disclaim all liability if any aspects of this book prove to be unreliable, incomplete, or inaccurate, or result in any losses.

This book and its contents are provided on an "as is" basis. Your use of the information in this book is at your own risk. Any perceived slight of any individual or organization is purely unintentional.

ISBN: 979-8-89109-296-9 - paperback

ISBN: 979-8-89109-297-6 - ebook

DOWNLOAD THE AUDIOBOOK FREE!

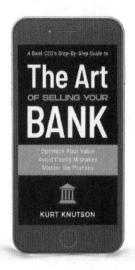

READ THIS FIRST

To say thank you for downloading my book, I would like to give you the Audiobook version 100% FREE!

I know you're more likely to finish this book if you have the audiobook.

I have even narrated the book myself so it will feel like we are having a conversation.

Instead of paying $10-$20 for the audiobook, I'd like to give it to you for free…

Go to: www. KurtKnutson.com/AudioBook

FREE BONUS CONTENT

Would you like access to free tools, videos, check-lists, and resources that were in development as this book went to press?

Go to: www.KurtKnutson.com/BonusContent

DEDICATION

MY FAMILY

To my wife Leanne

When we had kids who were 10 and 7 years old, she said "Go for it!" when I told her I was thinking about starting a bank. As the daughter of an entrepreneur, she understood the hours that were going to be necessary to get the bank started and operate it successfully.

To my kids, Katie and Jack, thank you for being the greatest kids a dad could have and thank you for being a part of the journey.

THE BOARD, SHAREHOLDERS, ADVISORY BOARD, CUSTOMERS AND EMPLOYEES OF FREEDOM BANK

Your investment in Freedom Bank helped support the vision, foresight, fortitude, and conviction to imagine a better way to deliver banking services to our community.

You stood by us through a financial crisis, a global pandemic, and when we were originally told what we were doing would never work.

We deployed one-half of a billion dollars in capital to local businesses in a fashion that challenged the status quo.

Our shareholders earned over 3.5x their original investment in what was the most difficult time to start and operate a bank in our nation's history.

You changed the lives of each other, our employees, shareholders, board, advisory board, and customers, both financially and professionally.

This is something few do. Even fewer understand.

Thank you for trusting us with your money and your careers.

TABLE OF CONTENTS

INTRODUCTION

"Strategy Without Tactics is the Slowest Route to Victory. Tactics Without Strategy is the Noise Before Defeat."
— SUN TZU

Every day as a bank CEO, you struggle to balance plates on sticks. Competitive threats, talent management, management succession, asset quality, liquidity, cybersecurity threats, interest rates, regulatory overreach, capital planning, along with customer and shareholder happiness are just a few of the plates on those sticks. You work feverishly to keep the plates spinning and balanced, so they don't fall.

In addition, you are continually scanning the horizon and keeping an eye out for potential strategic opportunities. Whether that's growing organically, acquiring, merging with a comparable sized bank, or selling outright, maximizing shareholder value is your primary obligation to the shareholders.

I believe that you will gain a clearer perspective of your strategic options by preparing as if you are selling, even if you have no plans to sell.

Why do I say that?

Selling your bank can make you feel like you're standing naked in public. The goal is to have your bank in the best shape possible, "swimsuit-ready" so to speak, at all times. By going through the process, you will also know when your bank is *not ready*, and *what it takes to get it ready*. You will be able to quiet the "noise" of the process which will calm your mind and allow you to concentrate on the correct plan.

The three big questions a CEO has when selling are:

- What is our value?
- Who is interested in buying us?
- What is the process?

Finding these answers is high-risk if word were to get out—you could lose customers and employees which could damage your earnings and ultimately your value.

Learning about the sales process is a road not often traveled due to the fear of being misunderstood. You might be concerned that the board will misinterpret your actions and conclude that you no longer have a passion for leading the company.

Confidentiality aside, asking an investment banker for guidance may seem like asking a barber if it's time for a haircut.

This book is meant to equip you with the resources you need so you can gain that peace of mind. You won't find a more streamlined collection of relevant information anywhere else.

The information supplied here forms the basis of a successful sales strategy—*even if the sales path is never taken.* The framework for a sale only enhances the understanding of your strategic options of growing organically, buying a bank, selling the bank, or merging with a bank of similar size.

Understanding the process will put you in a better position to make decisions. It will also serve as an aid for communicating your thoughts. Your strategy for allocating capital will improve. Fear of the unknown will go away. You will maximize shareholder value.

So how do I know this and how do I back up these assertions?

For the past four decades, I've been a banker, mostly a commercial banker focusing on working capital lines of credit, term loans, owner-occupied real estate, and cash management services.

For almost ten years, I was trained in and worked in capital markets and corporate finance. Banking and business ownership has been my life for the past 40 years.

Thanks to that background, I was able to successfully organize and lead a group of local businesspeople to raise the capital for a bank we founded in 2005.

In late 2021 into 2022, we went through the process outlined in this book. This book is not specific to our deal, nor is it a memoir. The information included in these pages is timeless.

We had a very successful sales process. The sale was good for everyone involved. The acquirer doubled their Kansas City loan portfolio, gaining a larger foothold in a faster-growth metro market (my words, not theirs) and added to their already strong presence throughout the rest of the state. Our shareholders received a return on their original investment that exceeded the S&P 500 over the duration of the investment. Our customers benefited from increased borrowing capacity and a wider range of products and services, and our employees have a much larger platform on which to continue their career growth. The buyer had over ten times the number of employees we had in 30 locations, offering our employees an opportunity to specialize in various areas of the bank.

I am not an investment banker, accountant, or lawyer, and I encourage you to always seek competent advice from professionals who know your situation.

I *am* proud to say that I am a banker who has been in your shoes. I have a tremendous respect for the profession and would like to give back by sharing what I've learned. This book will save you money, effort, and time. There are four decades of experience, involving a lot of late nights and weekends consuming information and putting it to the real-world test.

Use the knowledge provided to put your mind at ease. You will be in a much stronger position to express your ideas to the board, your team, and the shareholders after you shift your perspective on the available options. It will be easier to make decisions and convey ideas. Your strategy for allocating capital will improve. Fear of the unknown will be erased. You will maximize shareholder value and fulfill your fiduciary responsibilities of duty, loyalty, and care.

In 2017, we were eleven years old, our loan-to-deposit ratio was running consistently at 100%+, we had $40 million borrowed on our Federal Home Loan Bank (FHLB) line of credit and we had $60 million in bonds that we were holding an unrealized loss position in at the time.

The unexpected 2016 election results, regardless of your politics, had business owners reinvesting in their businesses. Loan demand was up. The business owners had newfound clarity on taxes, and wholesale deregulation was taking place, painting a very optimistic picture of the future for getting a return on their investment. Because of our loan funding needs and the increased loan demand, we decided to look at possibly acquiring a bank with a complementary balance sheet to fund our growth.

What that meant is that we were most likely looking at a rural bank who had been long-established, had a very diversified deposit base, and likely a low loan-to-deposit ratio (like 50%) because the kids perhaps had left the community for the growth of a metropolitan area. The diversified deposit base, with smaller average balances spread over many long-standing customers, would help offset the concentrations we had in larger average deposit balances having only been around for a relatively short number of years. If we could merge with a bank like that, we could loan the lower cost, diversified deposits, out in our market at a little bit higher spread. In exchange, we could supply management succession and IT expertise. We had developed a team of managers who were all under 40 years old who were high performing and would enjoy the opportunity to take on such a project.

The industry average age of bank management teams was 65 years of age. We knew our management succession would be important. The reason growth was low in those communities is because the younger generation had left.

We built a model, ran call reports through the model, and came up with a top 10 list of those we were interested in but had no idea if they had an interest in any such path. We began having introductory conversations on our own to see if we could begin any sort of relationship prior to bringing in an investment banker to assist us. The process moved into and through a good part of the summer of 2018.

In August of 2018, the bond market changed. We were able to get out of the $60 million we had tied up in bonds for a gain. Suddenly, we could pay down our $40 million FHLB line of credit and our balance sheet looked completely different. We needed to reanalyze and see if it changed the direction of who we may be interested in possibly acquiring.

We spent the first three quarters of 2019 running the bank and recalibrating the model. It did indeed give us a new top 10 list. Earnings became a more important factor along with a diversified deposit base and low loan-to-deposit ratio. That meant we were looking for a rural bank closer to a metropolitan area, possibly with a mortgage department and the associated fee income. We built our 2020 business plan around trying to build relationships with this new list. Then COVID hit. All conversations came to a halt. All banks were more concerned about whether we could survive. Businesses were being greatly impacted by COVID and we, along with everyone else, had no idea how long it would last. No one knew how catastrophic the loss of life would be—we'd never seen anything like it. We were prepared for it but had no idea on the extent to which it would reach. As 2020 closed out, the world had hoped the new vaccines would put an end to this horrible situation.

2021 began with a new-found optimism. Vaccines were going to begin in the first quarter. People began to slowly start to get together again in the second quarter. People were going to restaurants and ball games. Loan pipelines were beginning to fill up. Things seemed to finally be headed back to our pre-pandemic lives.

Then word of the Delta variant started to arise in the third quarter. That optimism became guarded. The loan pipelines remained full, but projects were delayed. We weren't quite through this yet. Our mergers and acquisitions (M&A) conversations were not ready to begin again. In the fourth quarter, we began preparing our 2022 business plan, and the Omicron variant began to appear.

As our board had conversations about 2022 and the potential plans to pick up on our acquisition strategy, we also broached the topic of our overall strategic options. Should we continue to grow organically, should we buy, should we sell, or perhaps should we even consider merging with a like-sized bank? We made the decision to see what those alternatives looked like and engaged an investment bank we had become very familiar with over the prior several years to assist us in weighing our options.

The point of this whole story is to provide context for you. We ended up selling when we were initially looking to acquire. It was a very successful process, and I have been in your chair and know the questions you have on your mind. The prior investment banking exposure in my background was an aid for me in going through the process. This is my opportunity to share the lessons learned along the way, so that you can gain exposure to it, learn from it, be familiar with it and ease your worries.

If you and the board ultimately want to sell, an investment banker can only work with the bank provided to them. It is very important to have the bank in a position to provide optimal value *before* handing it off to the investment banker. You don't want the regret of finding out the value drivers during the process and having to wonder, *What would our value have been if we could have known the process and changed a few things before we went down this path?*

Do not wait to continue reading this book. Get going right now on the framework suggested in Section 1. It's never too soon to get started. Keep the book close at hand as a resource while you work and put your own spin on the strategies and tactics it outlines.

My capital markets/corporate finance experience also allowed me to see the common problems that most business owners faced when it came time to sell their company. They lacked access to information and guidance, and they missed opportunities to prepare their company for sale and increase value for shareholders. In most cases, this preparation could have been done years earlier.

That lack of preparation usually results in finding only a single buyer and having no room to negotiate. It means leaving the worth of your bank and your story to chance.

By starting today, whether you intend to sell your bank or not, you will gain peace of mind knowing you put the bank on the right path towards meeting your fiduciary obligations. You will also leave a long-lasting legacy of your career.

The chapters in this book are the entire process organized in chronological order. The table of contents can be viewed as the process timeline.

SECTION 1

HOW MUCH
ARE WE WORTH?

CHAPTER 1

REVERSE ENGINEER

You know your bank better than anybody.

If you had a magic wand you could wave to buy another bank, what would the bank look like that you would want most?

What market(s) would it serve?

What products would it offer?

What would the deposit mix look like?

What would the loan portfolio mix look like?

What would the balance sheet look like?

Would it offer complementary services such as insurance, trust, leasing, or wealth management?

Would it offer additions to talent where gaps exist today?

Would it offer management succession where gaps exist today?

Would it have a more robust treasury services offering?

Would you want more shareholders, or would you want to pay cash?

Would you want more board members, or would you prefer not to add more complexity to your board?

Really think through this. Think through everything you would want and remember there is no cost to this—you have a magic wand you can wave to get exactly what you're looking for.

The exercise may be a bit eye opening, or you may have been thinking about this for quite some time and already know exactly what you'd want.

We were an acquirer in the years prior to our sale. We went through this process in detail. We built acquisition models and ran call reports through them to develop a top ten list. This analysis was very informative for us. It made us examine these questions from different angles. The analysis also made us examine ourselves. How far away would we be willing to go geographically to acquire? I got in the car and drove seven hours to a market we were considering. That trip made me realize that for us, that was too far. If we ever had problems in that market, the trip would make overseeing things more closely very difficult. We kept refining our scope the more we studied.

We were running hot. Our loan-to-deposit ratio was running consistently above 100%, we had $40 million borrowed on our Federal Home Loan Bank (FHLB) line of credit and we had $60 million in bonds with an unrealized loss position at the time. We were looking for a balance sheet that would complement ours. Low loan-to-value, a diversified deposit base built over years. We were a de novo about 10 years earlier, so our deposits naturally had concentrations. We were in a growing metropolitan market and finding a bank we could buy likely meant looking in a rural market. Rural market growth has been slowing over the years as the kids who grew up in those markets moved to larger markets for career opportunities. The parents remained in the rural markets and they had the deposits, but because the kids had left, there wasn't much growth.

Many rural banks lacked management depth for the same reason the growth was down in the market—those in the early stages of their careers had left for more opportunity elsewhere. Management at the rural banks was aging and succession planning was becoming an issue. We had recognized the demographic wave of retiring baby boomers during the early stages of our bank's existence. The bank was just a few years old; we couldn't afford to "buy" talent and we recognized we needed to develop the talent ourselves. That proved beneficial as the average age of our management team was 45 years old versus the industry average of 65 years old. *As a side note, at the time of our sale, I was 62 years old, and our president was 67 years old. We brought up the average age, and our team was all under the age of 40. We began the process of recruiting, hiring, and developing the team 13 years prior to our sale.*

So, in exchange for taking deposits from their slower-growth rural market and loaning them out in our higher-growth metropolitan market, we could be their management succession plan. In addition to that, information technology (IT) was typically something they would outsource, and our team was very comfortable with IT. We were looking for a combination that would make us both stronger. In other words, we were looking to make 2 + 2 = 5.

Our model was working exactly as planned. We had a top ten list we could focus on, and we began trying to have conversations with those on the list. We made progress, but the process takes time, and as time passes, things change. The bond market moved in our favor and the $60 million we had in bonds in an unrealized loss position previously now had gains. We cashed the bonds in and paid off the $40 million balance on our FHLB line of credit. Our balance sheet changed significantly, and our acquisition model was no longer valid. We needed to step back and reassess our needs and then recalibrate our acquisition model to fit our new circumstances.

We retooled the model and found we were still looking for a rural market bank for the same reasons mentioned previously, but we were now looking for a rural market bank a little closer geographically to a metropolitan market that had fee income as a part of their story. That fee income was typically derived from a residential mortgage function. We ran call reports through the model and developed another top ten list. As we set out to begin contacting our prospect list, COVID hit.

There were no acquisition conversations during COVID. No one knew how catastrophic the loss of lives would be—we had never seen anything like this. We were all just trying to figure out if our customers and our bank would survive. As a bank, we were prepared for a pandemic but had no idea how long it would last. So, for a period of two years, we stayed focused on our organic growth plans. As we began to make plans for 2022, the board discussed acquisitions. This time, however, in addition to our conversations about buying another bank, we also talked about whether we would have an interest in selling to another bank. It had been four years since we began the process of looking to buy a bank. Enough time had passed that the board decided to explore whether there was an interest in our bank, if for nothing else, to point out where we needed to refine or enhance to increase our value.

That conversation led us to the first question on everybody's mind: What's our value?

We had a stock valuation done for us by an independent third party every year, but it was per share value for a minority interest and was likely pretty conservative to fit the risk profile of the appraisers. What would we really be worth in a "live" sale environment?

To close this chapter, the process we went through to find who we might be interested in buying was very instructive. We were bought by a bank that was roughly 6 times our size and they were much like the banks we modeled acquiring. Predominately in rural markets, great deposit base, lower loan-to-deposit ratio looking for additional growth in a metropolitan market to build value for the franchise overall (these are my words and thoughts, not theirs, as I cannot speak for them).

The process of figuring out who would complement us led us to becoming more familiar with our own value. The process, reverse engineered, was very instructive as to the value we could bring to somebody else. We will be going into this further here in Section 1, but I would highly recommend that you consider the elements in a bank you would look to hypothetically acquire that would make it a $2 + 2 = 5$ combination for you. It will be more instructive and valuable for you than the time it takes to dedicate your thoughts to, and I believe this will become clearer to you as you make your way through the book.

WHAT TO EXPECT FROM THIS BOOK

This book is designed to be a practical guide and reference tool based on real-world experience. My goal is that this book will become your go-to guide and answer your questions if you are considering selling your bank.

This book is not a replacement for an investment banker. They bring an immense amount of value that will be discussed throughout the book. Nor is this book a replacement for your legal counsel or accountant. This book is written from the perspective of a banker in a CEO-to-CEO type of conversation.

The content of this book applies regardless of the size of your bank; however, I will concede there is a stronger correlation to banks with total assets between $100 million to $2 billion.

The chapters in this book are the entire process organized in chronological order. The table of contents can be viewed as the process timeline.

CHAPTER 2

REFOCUS PERSPECTIVE

A fter going through the reverse engineering process to find the right fit for an acquisition with us as a buyer, and then making the decision to see if the market was possibly interested in us, we had to refocus our perspective to that of a seller.

I believe it is human nature for a business owner, any business—it doesn't have to be a bank—to mentally think, "Okay, if we're going to sell, here's what we have. You can see our history, what are you willing to pay me for it?" Or, more simply put, "Here's what I have, what do I get?"

There's a natural tendency to flip a switch in your mind where you no longer have to think about the future of the business—after all, that's the *buyer's* concern following the sale. To some extent, that is true, but it assumes the seller receives full cash consideration at closing. They are paid in full. That may be the case, but it may not. Perhaps the buyer wants to use their stock to buy the bank, or a combination of cash and their stock.

Until the sale has been completed, meaning the seller has no future payments at risk, there is still a great deal of thinking about the future that must take place.

Here's the hardest part: thinking about the buyer's future with your business as a part of it.

Buyers are interested in what the future holds of the combination—what they can do with your business added in and what they can become. And at this point you don't know how the market values your bank, you don't know the terms of the deal, and you don't know if it will be an all-cash deal, a stock deal, or a cash and stock combination.

So, the mindset needs to shift from "Have & Get" to "Do & Become."

The main takeaway here is that the buyer is looking out the front window of the car towards the future—the road ahead. The seller is often looking in the rearview mirror of where the company has been.

As bankers, we have spent our whole careers judging businesses by looking in the rearview mirror. We look for steady, repeatable, predictable cash flow. Cash is the only thing that repays loans. Sure, we want projections so we can understand what a borrower is trying to do in the future, but we don't get paid for the risk of betting on untested projected cash flow. Equity investors are the ones looking out the front window, taking the risk on future projected cash flows. They get paid for taking the risk.

So, it is important to note that a refocus of perspective is needed here. It is more important now than ever before to think about the future. It's just really difficult because it is *somebody else's* future.

Two last things to note here: You don't know who the eventual buyer could be, so not only do you have to think about somebody else's future, you might have to think of multiple parties' futures at the same time. And, when the sale does eventually happen, just because you go through the process thinking about the future of the buyer with your bank added in—that future direction is not your call anymore.

The ultimate buyer may go down the path you have painted for the reason your bank is so valuable to them. But they might not. The importance to you of that factor will likely depend on whether you are paid in cash, a cash and stock combination or all stock. The ideal answer is up to your board, and ultimately, your shareholders.

If you receive cash consideration, the future risk is shouldered by the buyer completely. If you receive stock consideration, your shareholders are sharing in the risk, and those conversations about the future should be well understood before continuing. Your input as to the future of the combined banks will slide on a cash and stock combination depending on the balance between the two.

We're going to get into more specifics of what is meant by a "Do & Become" mindset in our future chapters.

CHAPTER 3

WHAT ARE YOUR EARNINGS IF...?

O kay, we need to begin refocusing our perspective to "Do & Become." As mentioned in the last chapter, we don't know the party we are thinking about, and we don't have a clear view of the future as a combined bank. But we do have enough to start putting information together that will be common to the parties interested in buying us.

Historical bank M&A data indicates that a buyer will likely be in the range of five to seven times your size. So, just for perspective, let's say your bank has $250 million in total assets. Your potential buyer will likely be in the range of $1.2 billion to $1.8 billion. If you're a $100 million bank, your potential buyer would be in the range of $500 million to $700 million.

If we can get an idea of the *size* of a potential acquirer, we can extrapolate an *estimate of what the legal lending limit* would be for that bank. That's good information to consider. You likely have borrowers in your loan portfolio that are at your internal hold limit or even perhaps at your legal lending limit. And you know the borrowers well enough that if you had a higher internal hold limit or legal lending limit, you would have no problem extending additional credit to them.

You might have sold participations to others because of your internal hold limits or legal lending limits as well. Look at those participations sold. You may want to purchase them back if you have the capacity. My guess is that you want those earnings if you now could hold those loans. You've already made the credit decision. Start building a list, by customer, of those who would have a larger relationship with you if you were five to seven times the size you are today.

In addition, you may be able to add to your leasing portfolio if you have more capital and a higher legal lending limit. Or, if there were considerably more locations that you would have as a part of a larger organization, perhaps your mortgage unit could expand, and you could increase the number of loans closed and fees earned.

The whole point here is to think "Do & Become."

You don't know who the potential buyer could be, so don't try to predict what they might or might not be interested in. Just think of your bank being five to seven times its size and make some assumptions on additional locations and imagine what you could do with that.

As previously mentioned, the buyer is under no obligation to execute the plan you are coming up with, but it helps to go through the process of thinking through this and building out assumptions so that you can help paint a picture of *what could be.*

It can't be assumed that the potential buyer has the imagination to understand what could be in your customer base and product mix. It is up to the buyer to execute the plan they build for the acquisition. That is their risk to manage. Execution risk.

These are exercises only you can do. Investment bankers can't do this for you. Only *you* will know this information.

They can only work with what is provided to them. Stay highly engaged.

In the next chapter, we're going to take the assumptions made and translate them into potential future earnings in our journey to find out how much we're worth.

CHAPTER 4

LONG-TERM PLAN

We've reverse engineered a complementary balance sheet that fits with ours. We've decided to see if the market has a desire to buy our bank, and we're refocusing our perspective on what the future may look like for a buyer who is five to seven times our size. We've thought about how much bigger our loan portfolio would be just within our existing customer base. The next step is to build a set of projections for the next five years. That may sound like an unpleasant experience. Your first thought might be, "I'm going to need to get more people on board." But hold on! It doesn't have to be very complicated.

It's actually very simple to put together.

Have five years (or more if you'd prefer) of your historical numbers for the following three variables:

- Total Assets
- Capital
- Earnings

Next, you can easily build the following calculations into your spreadsheet with the three variables entered:

- Return on Assets (ROA)
- Capital to Assets
- Asset Growth

Your spreadsheet will look like this (For those listening to the audiobook please go to www.KurtKnutson.com/BonusContent for the worksheet referenced here):

	A	B	C	D	E	F	G	H
1	**Year**	**Assets**	**Earnings**	**Capital**	**ROA**	**Capital/ Assets**	**Asset Growth**	**% Growth**
2	Historical Year 1							
3	Historical Year 2							
4	Historical Year 3							
5	Historical Year 4							
6	Historical Year 5							
7	Current Year							
8	Projected Year 1							
9	Projected Year 2							
10	Projected Year 3							
11	Projected Year 4							
12	Projected Year 5							

This is a simple spreadsheet, but it does the job, and it does it well. It doesn't mean the underlying assumptions aren't thought through—quite the contrary. The underlying assumptions are what you'll need to spend some time thinking about and will need to defend, but you don't need to enlist the assistance of anybody else at this point to get the spreadsheet built.

I would recommend you consider using this as your guide every year and build a spreadsheet just based on your operation without selling being considered. This is a great way for you to look at what the performance of the bank should be from year-to-year without the "noise" of how you get there. It's just math. Your team can then look at how they will achieve the outcome, as long as they are included in the purpose of the Long-Term Plan and are shown it (at least) annually. The team is responsible for coming up with a plan to hit the numbers. The team executes the plan, you, and ultimately the board, approve the plan. Then take that spreadsheet and build in your *sale scenario*, that way you'll have a base set of assumptions and will be able to overlay your sale scenario on those base assumptions.

Let's walk through this.

You've gathered your historical data. It could be you just pulled up your call reports right from the FDIC website, could be you have your financials. Either way, you should have ready access to the numbers you need.

The cells shaded gray are the cells you are going to put your historical data or your assumptions in. The cells that are not shaded are the cells that will contain your formulas. For those listening to the audiobook please go to www.KurtKnutson.com/BonusContent for the worksheet referenced here.

	A	B	C	D	E	F	G	H
1	Year	Assets	Earnings	Capital	ROA	Capital/Assets	Asset Growth	% Growth
2	Historical Year 1	(historical)	(historical)	(historical)	=C2/B2	=D2/B2	--	--
3	Historical Year 2	(historical)	(historical)	(historical)	=C3/B3	=D3/B3	=B3-B2	=G3/B2
4	Historical Year 3	(historical)	(historical)	(historical)	=C4/B4	=D4/B4	=B4-B3	=G4/B3
5	Historical Year 4	(historical)	(historical)	(historical)	=C5/B5	=D5/B5	=B5-B4	=G5/B4
6	Historical Year 5	(historical)	(historical)	(historical)	=C6/B6	=D6/B6	=B6-B5	=G6/B5
7	Current Year	=B6+G7	=B7*E7	=D6+C7	(assumption)	=D7/B7	(assumption)	=G7/B6
8	Projected Year 1	=B7+G8	=B8*E8	=D7+C8	(assumption)	=D8/B8	(assumption)	=G8/B7
9	Projected Year 2	=B8+G9	=B9*E9	=D8+C9	(assumption)	=D9/B9	(assumption)	=G9/B8
10	Projected Year 3	=B9+G10	=B10*E10	=D9+C10	(assumption)	=D10/B10	(assumption)	=G10/B9
11	Projected Year 4	=B10+G11	=B11*E11	=D10+C11	(assumption)	=D11/B11	(assumption)	=G11/B10
12	Projected Year 5	=B11+G12	=B12*E12	=D11+C12	(assumption)	=D12/B12	(assumption)	=G12/B11

Let's look at the same spreadsheet with the assumptions built in and the formulas having made calculations based on the assumptions for our mythical bank: ACME Bank. For those listening to the audiobook please go to www. KurtKnutson.com/BonusContent for the worksheet referenced here.

	A	B	C	D	E	F	G	H
1	Year	Assets	Earnings	Capital	ROA	Capital/Assets	Asset Growth	% Growth
2	2018	$103,000,000	$724,000	$8,441,361	0.70%	7.47%	--	--
3	2019	$123,000,000	$804,000	$9,245,361	0.65%	7.52%	$20,000,000	19.42%
4	2020	$132,000,000	$1,152,000	$10,397,361	0.87%	7.88%	$9,000,000	7.32%
5	2021	$147,000,000	$1,565,000	$11,962,361	1.06%	8.14%	$15,000,000	11.36%
6	2022	$164,000,000	$1,567,800	$13,350,161	0.96%	8.25%	$17,000,000	11.56%
7	2023	$184,000,000	$1,674,400	$15,204,561	0.91%	8.26%	$20,000,000	12.20%
8	2024	$206,000,000	$1,915,800	$17,120,361	0.93%	8.31%	$22,000,000	11.96%
9	2025	$233,000,000	$2,027,100	$19,147,461	0.87%	8.22%	$27,000,000	13.11%
10	2026	$258,000,000	$2,373,600	$21,521,061	0.92%	8.34%	$25,000,000	10.73%
11	2027	$286,000,000	$2,745,600	$24,266,661	0.96%	8.48%	$28,000,000	10.85%
12	2028	$316,000,000	$3,160,000	$27,426,661	1.00%	8.68%	$30,000,000	10.49%

Here are the assumptions behind the numbers above:

- Don't get caught up on the actual years listed above. For these purposes, the years are just hypothetical and COVID did not happen. (That's just noise for the principles here. This example is just for illustration of how to put this spreadsheet together).

- Again, the grayed boxes for Assets, Earnings, and Capital are actuals (hypothetical here). The grayed boxes for ROA and Asset Growth will be addressed shortly.

- General assumptions are for illustration only. This is a healthy bank—strong asset quality in a healthy economy, and the bank is in a higher-growth metropolitan market.

- The grayed boxes for ROA and Asset Growth are what drive the spreadsheet for the current year and future years, so this is where you need to devote most of your thoughts:

  o ROA assumptions: Look at the historical average of your bank and the trend. Think about what the drivers behind the numbers are. What are the drivers of the trend? Also think about what initiatives you have in mind for the future and how that might affect the assumptions.

    ▪ For ACME's ROA assumptions: The last five-year average was 0.85%. The trend is headed up. An additional seasoned commercial lender was added in Q4 of 2022, so that lender will have additional expense and will begin contributing in 2023. For these reasons, a more conservative number was used for ROA in 2023. Also, if your bank has fee income, remember that is contemplated in the ROA.

- There weren't any additional lenders added in 2024, and it is contemplated that the lender added in 2022 is now contributing at a higher level.

- In 2024, two additional commercial relationship managers are contemplated being added, so the 2025 ROA is backed off to 0.87%. One could do the same by adding a branch, a new function such as mortgage banking, insurance, wealth management, or trust. Those would all be reflected in the ROA assumptions.

- The 2026-2028 ROA assumptions are trending up as the two additional relationship managers are contributing to a greater degree each year.

- As a side note, 2018 & 2019 ROA numbers were impacted by the addition of new computer systems integrations, more one-time upfront expense was incurred in those years.

■ Asset growth assumptions match the relationship manager additions contemplated in the ROA assumptions above.

- Historical asset growth averaged $15,250,000 (2018 growth was not included as it serves as the base year for our spreadsheet, but you could add that if you have the prior year's number).

- There was a drop-off in asset growth in 2020 due to the relationship managers portfolios growing to a point of diminishing returns. Too many relationships spread between too few relationship managers dampened calling activity.

- The number of commercial relationship managers was four (4) in 2022 and is projected to be seven (7) by the end of 2028.

- Loan growth is projected to be 12.2% in 2023, 11.96% in 2024, 13.11% in 2025, 10.73% in 2026 and may flatten a bit to 10.85% in 2027 and 10.49% in 2028. The percentage increases are defensible given historical performance and are supported by the previously mentioned assumptions.

That should give you a pretty good level of understanding of how the spreadsheet can be used as a tool and the thought process behind the assumptions. This forms the basis for the building of the "Do & Become" earnings projections in a sale scenario.

Here are our assumptions for building the hypothetical sales projections for our fictional ACME Bank:

- The general assumptions for ACME remain the same. For illustration simplicity, this is a healthy bank with a strong asset quality, it's a healthy economy, and the bank is in a higher-growth metropolitan market.

- The acquiring bank is five to seven times the size of ACME and ACME's assets for the year most recently completed were $164 million. So, the acquirer would be assumed to be in the total asset range of $800 million to $1.2 billion (5 x $161 million = $820 million; 7 x $161 million = $1.148 billion).

- For assumption purposes, the acquisition takes place in Q2 of 2024.

- ACME's CEO, Bill Jones, has gone through the loan portfolio and has determined between relationships that could extend beyond the current legal lending limit and the current internal hold limit with some participations sold being repurchased and some relationships that could extend beyond the current list of customers because of a greater reach. And $30,000,000 in additional loan fundings could be added to the portfolio beginning in 2024 with $15,000,000 and the additional $15,000,000 added to the 2025 numbers.

- Additional treasury services fee income has been increased as well as relationships are added and expanded.

- Keeping the percentage of growth numbers, the same as in the organic growth projection previously built of 11.96% in 2024, 13.11% in 2025, 10.73% in 2026, 10.85% in 2027, 10.49% in 2028 and adding an additional year of 10.5% in 2029 so there are five years of projections post-acquisition.

- Assuming the back-office support and scalability is in place to support the growth.

- Capital to Assets for **_our_** projection purposes does not matter (N/A). We are assuming the capital of the acquirer can absorb the acquisition with room to grow.

- We are assuming an expense reduction of 35% with that all beginning in 2025, so our ROA number reflects that.

Here is our post-sale projection model for ACME BANK (And again, for those listening to the audiobook please go to www.KurtKnutson.com/BonusContent for the worksheet referenced here):

	A	B	C	D	E	F	G	H
1	Year	Assets	Earnings	Capital	ROA	Capital/Assets	Asset Growth	% Growth
2	2018	$103,000,000	$724,000	$8,441,361	0.70%	7.47%	--	--
3	2019	$123,000,000	$804,000	$9,245,361	0.65%	7.52%	$20,000,000	19.42%
4	2020	$132,000,000	$1,152,000	$10,397,361	0.87%	7.88%	$9,000,000	7.32%
5	2021	$147,000,000	$1,565,000	$11,962,361	1.06%	8.14%	$15,000,000	11.36%
6	2022	$164,000,000	$1,567,800	$13,350,161	0.96%	8.25%	$17,000,000	11.56%
7	2023	$184,000,000	$1,674,400	$15,204,561	0.91%	8.26%	$20,000,000	12.20%
8	2024	$221,000,000	$2,055,300	$17,259,861	0.93%	7.81%	$37,000,000	20.11%
9	2025	$264,966,019	$3,312,075	$20,571,936	1.25%	7.76%	$43,966,019	19.89%
10	2026	$293,395,850	$3,814,146	$24,386,082	1.30%	8.31%	$28,429,830	10.73%
11	2027	$325,237,260	$4,553,322	$28,939,404	1.40%	8.90%	$31,841,410	10.85%
12	2028	$359,353,056	$5,390,296	$34,329,700	1.50%	9.55%	$34,115,796	10.49%
13	2029	$397,085,127	$6,353,362	$40,683,062	1.60%	10.25%	$37,732,071	10.50%

You may be looking at the numbers and are tempted to bring them down a bit. Resist that temptation! This is a point where I would highly encourage using investment bankers. Particularly "bank sell-side" investment bankers who have a lot of "deal experience." Walk through the logic with your investment bankers before you have any thoughts about giving this a haircut and making it more conservative.

Only you can perform this initial exercise. Your investment bankers don't know what you can do with additional lending capacity. They can only build off what is given to them. If you don't actively participate in this, you are likely to leave money on the table.

Your investment bankers will want to have a good enough feel about the assumptions you have given them so that it is defensible in their conversations with the "buy-side" investment bankers. If you get too conservative, which we as bankers do, you will be getting a conservative number knocked down further and end up leaving money on the table.

Again, all the above is hypothetical based on a mythical bank and an assumed buyer. The point is you need to let your mind go to this place.

At this point, you might be thinking "I don't know if this will be a cash deal, a stock deal, or a cash plus stock deal." You are also likely wondering if you will be responsible for the results and are beginning to get a dry mouth thinking about it.

Resist the urge to dwell on this. It's too early. If you go through this process earnestly, your answers will be defensible too.

The assumptions we just went through are not off the wall. They are defensible.

You want to look at it as if you are going to be responsible for delivering those results.

<u>What you don't control, however, is the buyer's ability to execute on the strategy—in fact, you don't even know what their strategy is.</u>

It's too early for that.

Anchor your number on the upper end. You can always move down if need be. Once you lower your price, you won't be able to move up.

If it's an all-stock deal, you will need to have the buyer's business plan shared with you because you are going to share in the execution risk. You will also share in the execution risk of a cash/stock combination. As such, the business plan may be shared to a degree relative to the execution risk you will be sharing. In an all-cash deal, you may not even see the business plan. The execution risk is taken on by the buyer in that event. The ideal answer as to whether it's an all-cash offer, a stock offer, or a combination of the two is up to the offer(s) you do, in fact, receive. If you don't get any all-cash offers, it need not be factored in. The same holds true for all-stock offers or combination offers. If you receive all three types, the all-stock offer or the stock/cash combination offer should be higher than the all-cash offer because of the execution risk your shareholders will be assuming. The ultimate answer is up to your directors and your shareholders once you have done your offer comparison analysis.

So again, it's too early.

Let's keep moving forward and talk about determining value.

CHAPTER 5

DETERMINING VALUE

W hen we talk about finding a bank valuation in this context, we are talking about the _sale value_ of selling the _whole bank_. This is where the rubber meets the road.

While each bank is unique, the beauty is often in the eye of the beholder. Buyers and sellers disagree on price in nearly every negotiation. So, let's go through the different methods for determining the sale value of a bank (whether you are selling now or in the future, or not selling).

To gain an understanding of the methods used to estimate sales value, we are going to focus on the variables that might positively drive sale value as well as variables that might detract or negatively drive sales value.

Most start with multiples. They are a shortcut and don't require much thought other than a quick calculation. Keep this in mind when using multiples. For illustration, let's compare the results of the sale of two banks, both selling at the same time. They both have $200 million in assets, and both are selling for $30 million.

The only difference between the two is that the first bank has tangible common equity of 8%, and the second bank has tangible common equity of 11%. So, the first bank has tangible common equity of $16 million. The second bank has tangible common equity of $22 million. For the purposes of illustration, this is the only difference between the two banks, and it is just driven by the capital policy of each board.

The price to tangible book value (TBV) multiple of the first bank is 1.88x.

The price to TBV multiple of the second bank is 1.36x.

If you are thinking that the first bank deployed its capital more efficiently and is being rewarded with a higher multiple because of that efficiency, you may be correct. But let's add another consideration into the mix.

The first bank had a return on assets (ROA) of 0.5%, earning a net income of $1 million. The second bank had an ROA of 1%, or net income of $2 million (and one could argue that the capital held in the bank was higher as a result).

The price to earnings (P/E) multiple for the first bank was 30x and the P/E for the second bank was 15x.

So, logically, the owners of the second bank would think before all of this took place that they should get a higher multiple than the first bank when selling their bank in comparison. In their minds they earn more and have a better capitalized bank. That means they believe their bank has more value.

Multiples are really the result of a sale transaction, AFTER the arrival of the sales value.

Most shareholders could care less about the multiples. They want the highest price per share they can get so they can maximize the return on the use of their money for the time it was being used. Period. And, from a corporate finance perspective, they are exactly right.

To borrow from Aswath Damodaran, professor of Finance at the Stern School of Business at New York University, we need to understand why delving into the details of valuation is important. He illustrates his point by telling the story of the lemmings.

The lemmings became famous, or infamous, when they appeared in a 1958 Disney documentary called White Wilderness. The lemmings appeared to have gathered on a cliff and ran off the cliff into the ocean to their deaths. The question that arose was, "Why did they do it? Why did they commit collective suicide?"

You can see the first lemming in your mind, right? He was going too fast; he couldn't stop, and he went right off the cliff.

The second lemming was too close to the first lemming and the same thing happened.

Put yourself in the shoes of that very last lemming.

You're going as fast as you can to the edge of a cliff. You've seen the entire tribe disappear off that cliff. I would assume you would have second thoughts about what you're planning to do.

But then you hear a voice in the back of your head saying…

"They must know something I don't."

Remember those six words. <u>They are the deadliest words in investing</u>.

Do you know when you hear them?

When you value a company.

Damodaran's example goes on to divide the lemmings into three groups.

- Proud lemmings
- Yogi Bear lemmings
- Life Vest lemmings

Proud lemmings are momentum investors. They look for a crowd. They join in. When you're buying, I'm buying. When you're selling, I'm selling. Why are you buying? Why are you selling? I don't care.

If you've ever seen the old Yogi Bear cartoons, you probably remember his most famous expression – "I'm smarter than the average bear!"

Yogi Bear lemmings think they're smarter than the average lemming.

They run with the crowd until they get to the very edge of the cliff and at the last moment veer away.

Yogi Bear lemmings are market-timers. They feel they are smarter than the other lemmings and they'll be able to know when it's the "right time" to get in or out.

If you can pull that off, that's great. You get all the upside and none of the downside.

That's nearly impossible, if not impossible, to do without blind luck.

Valuation gives you a life vest. It gives you something to hold onto when everybody goes in the same direction or when everyone else changes their minds.

That's a Life Vest lemming. If you really, really want to buy something, you're going to find a way to buy it. If you really want to sell something, you're going to find a way to sell.

Valuation slows the process down.

It gives your rational side time to mount an argument.

That's why valuation is important.

The three big reasons the valuation process breaks down is when the person doing the valuation incorrectly concludes, it's not about the numbers, it's not about the models, and it's not about the metrics. *"I know what the company is worth."*

The biggest problem is that most people sit down to value a company or business and they already have a *preconceived value* they are expecting to see.

<u>The great irony is the more you know about a company, the stronger those preconceptions are, and when those preconceptions get set, your valuation follows</u>.

In general, a composite of several valuation approaches will likely yield the most valid basis in which to form your conclusions.

So, we've already discussed the <u>first valuation approach</u>, which could be called the **drive-by approach**, not much in terms of in-depth analysis—just *multiples*, and in particular, just *price to tangible book value*.

The <u>second valuation approach</u> is the next-door neighbor to multiples because it uses the price to tangible book value multiple and the not-so-scientific approach of the "We're a better bank than that so our multiple must be higher" otherwise known as the **competitive approach**. Our people are better, or we beat them all the time in head-to-head competition, or they don't know what they're doing. We are worth more than them.

The third approach is starting to gather actual data, so it is more scientific than the first two approaches—recent comparable transactions—or the **relative value approach**. You look at similar banks that have been priced in the market right now. Try looking at 10 recent transactions of comparable sized banks in comparable sized markets with similar performance ratios, almost like a peer group analysis. As those who loan on real estate are aware, appraisals use the comparable sales approach. You must really study the differences in the properties being used for comparison to get a valid understanding of the value you are measuring.

By using approaches one (drive-by), two (competitive), or three (relative), the analyst is essentially saying, "Anything beyond these approaches is too complicated. I'm going to let the market tell me." You may not be able to compare the values of individual banks because some are smaller and some are larger, but if you divide that value by earnings and book value, in other words use a multiple, you are essentially comparing numbers that are comparable. Finding a bank that looks just like yours might be easy or it might be tough to do. Typically, when there is difficulty finding a comparison, the analyst ultimately ends up saying, "You know what? They're probably not that comparable."

The fourth approach is the **intrinsic value approach**. Now we're getting more specific relative to the bank being valued. We're valuing the bank on its fundamentals, its cash flows, its growth, and its risk. At its core, the value should be a function of the bank's future cash flows. This ties back to "Do & Become" discussed earlier. What price should I pay now in relation to the returns I am going to get in the future? This also ties back to the Long-Term Plan discussion just prior to this—a five-year projection of future income with cost savings factored in—to arrive at the cash flows over the next five years, then for perpetuity through a terminal value. In a discounted cash flow valuation, the value of an asset is the present value of the expected cash flows of the asset. Nothing more, nothing less. Discounted cash flow analysis is the most common tool used for estimating intrinsic value, but it's not the only one. But the key to intrinsic value is it's all about that bank.

The hidden ingredient for using discounted cash flow valuation is you need a long-time horizon. Because markets can make mistakes. You can find those mistakes, but there is no guarantee that those mistakes will get corrected in the next three months or six months or even a year. The longer the time horizon, the better off you are using a discounted cash flow valuation. Keep that in mind when preparing the Long-Term Plan projections discussed earlier. When the transaction closes, the execution risk and the time horizon are transferred to the buyer. Your Long-Term Plan projections will be the foundation for performing the discounted cash flow analysis. That discounted cash flow analysis is preferably done by your investment banker, which is another very strong reason why hiring an investment banker is a good idea and money well spent.

The fifth approach is the **ability to pay** ("ATP") approach. The thought behind this approach is what the buyer is willing and able to pay for the seller. The buyer's ability and willingness to pay is really a function of two factors: strategic interest, which is totally subjective, and financial considerations which are more objective. An example would be if you're a collector, and there is a specific item missing from your collection. You may be willing to pay above and beyond the market value for that one item because when it completes your collection, your collection increases by greater value than your above market payment for the one piece.

Strategic buyers are encouraged to inwardly examine what's important to them well before they think about a deal, so they can map those criteria up against a potential target. That can be anything, it's subjective and at the whim of the board and the management team, from operating scale and market share diversification to human capital or what have you. We will be discussing strategic considerations in detail in Chapter 8 – Strategic Value and Chapter 9 – Talent.

The financial side is easier to consider as it is more objective than subjective. That's the other box that ought to get checked by the buyer in advance of an acquisition.

A savvy seller can reverse engineer how buyers will look at these established financial criteria that they use to calculate their ability to pay. That's exactly what you should consider doing, whether you are selling or not._

Reverse engineer a buyer's ability to pay? How do you do that?

Well, using a very detailed, complicated pro forma model you can develop, you can overlay what you uncover against some relatively easy, common acquisition criteria. There are usually three or four criteria and most, if not all, savvy buyers that have a track record of adding value for their shareholders through acquisitions, use these metrics. *This is another reason why I would highly recommend using a good investment banker, one that specializes in bank sell-side transactions of banks of similar size to yours. They understand the individual buyer's acquisition criteria—they are living in that world every day and having conversations with the buyers on a regular basis.*

Common acquisition criteria are…

Number one, **earnings per share**. Specifically, what impact will this acquisition have on my earnings per share going forward?

Number two, what kind of **internal rate of return** will I get?

Number three, buyers will look at what level of **tangible book value per share dilution** will be realized and **how long it takes to earn that back**.

And then **finally**, savvy buyers will look at **capital levels**. Where does this leave me in terms of capital? Do I need incremental borrowings or common or preferred equity to finance this acquisition? Are there associated costs that need to be factored in?

There's generally a range a buyer has for each of these criteria. Some buyers might be willing to go to the high end of the range, some might be willing to go to the low end of the range. *But in short, with the help of a good sell-side investment banker, you can reverse engineer a model to basically identify a pretty good range of what most buyers would be willing and able to pay for that bank.*

So, what do we do with all that?

You look at a grid of the valuation ranges produced by the analyses.

What I am referring to is a grid of the various methodologies, laid out side-by-side, adding insight into a range of values a buyer may be expected to pay or may have the ability to pay.

Once the grid is built, you will have a quick visual map of the *ranges* calculated for the following valuation metrics:

- Comparable Transactions
  - o Net Income
  - o Net Income Plus Cost Savings
  - o Tangible Book Value
  - o Total Assets
  - o Core Deposit Premium
- Discounted Cash Flows
- Ability to Pay Analysis

This is the "**science**" part of the analysis. This is the outline of a picture that is beginning to come together of your value.

The "**art**" of the analysis is what comes next.

The art is an overlay of *market color*—what is happening at the time you are doing your analysis—or the color that adds to your picture of valuation giving it further definition and detail.

Your understanding of the market and what is taking place within the market is limited, no matter how much you think you're on top of it. That's just a fact.

This is where an investment banker's understanding of bank M&A market conditions is extremely valuable for dialing in the range you might be expected to realize in a sale or might be expecting to pay in the event you are a buyer. At the risk of beating a dead horse, the investment banker is actively engaged in that world daily. They don't get paid unless they are successful—they eat what they kill.

They are dialed in, but you need to understand that they have limits on doing analyses that don't pay in the long run.

They are very interested in providing value to you outside of an engagement so that when you are ready for an engagement you consider choosing them. We will discuss choosing an investment banker in more detail in Chapter 12 – Building the Advisor Team.

The overlay they add is the art detail you just can't provide in your own analysis: What they're seeing in the marketplace in real-time, based on the deal flow they're seeing, on the conversations they're having, knowledge of the buyers, and market demand.

You can, nevertheless, apply your understanding of what is happening in the world of bank M&A to your analysis. Your analysis is very valuable because you are sharpening your understanding of the drivers of your bank's value.

Let's look in further detail at those drivers.

CHAPTER 6

VALUE DRIVERS

What drives value, and what detracts from it?

This is not an exhaustive list, but it is the most significant.

First, we'll look at **five primary value drivers** that influence value.

By far the most important value driver is **core earnings**. These are earnings that are consistent, dependable, and predictable. These earnings are resulting from the core business of the bank. So, the duller the trend of core earnings, being the same or growing consistently every year, creates value better than anything.

The second value driver is **cost savings** or expense reduction, often referred to as "synergies." It's very straightforward. You take two existing banks and combine them to cut expenses. All else being equal, the new bank will be far more profitable than either of the two independently. The greater the number of expenses that may be decreased, the greater the value. We will cover the core contract in a little more added detail in Chapter 10 – The Golden Window.

The third value driver is **core growth**. This has the same properties as core earnings. This growth is coming from the core business of the bank. This is consistent, dependable, and predictable growth. It doesn't have to be at the same rate of growth every year, but consistent, dependable, and predictable growth in both loans and deposits create value.

The fourth value driver is **credit quality**. Credit quality is expected in the world of bank mergers and acquisitions. It drives value, but the value is expected to be there, because no one pays a premium for a high-quality loan portfolio. What it does is prevent price declines. High credit quality is expected—it's treated as a given.

The final value driver mentioned here is **talent**. Savvy bank buyers will flat out tell you they aren't interested in buying the bank if it is the selling bank's management team's desire is to retire at closing. They are unfamiliar with your bank. They are unfamiliar with your market or your people. There's a lot more value if you're willing to stick around for a year, three years, or five years to make the transaction work.

Talent beyond management is a value driver if key employees, particularly customer-facing employees, have Stay-Put provisions already in place. It reduces the risk that they may not stay if control changes, and the buyer must negotiate the agreements. Other employees who may not be bound by Stay-Put agreements but solve succession planning needs the buyer has or can serve in another role that is needed also can enhance value.

There are also *value detractors* that would-be sellers should be aware of.

The first value detractor is **non-core earnings**. A good example may be cold loan participation earnings. Loans where the bank is blind to the customer and *there is no other relationship other than the loan participation*. You likely have never had a conversation with the borrower, only working through the lead participant to get information or financials. That income was basically worthless in terms of value. It contributed to book value, but it is considered "one-time" earnings by the buyer that will not be repeated. A one-time gain on the sale of securities, other real estate owned (OREO), or non-core earnings do not generate value.

Non-core growth is a value detractor as well. This is also a scenario in which value is not generated. Wholesale CDs, the proceeds of which are used to buy wholesale bonds, inflate the balance sheet. There's a money-making spread play there. There is a favorable spread, but it is not indicative of core growth. Non-core growth will detract from value. There is no relationship behind that growth. You are just buying this business. Anybody can buy it. You bring no value proposition to this business.

The third value detractor is **large one-time transaction costs**. These expenses can reduce value. A long period remaining on a data processing contract is one example. The first thing you should do is look up your core contract expiration date. What is the termination fee if you decide to leave before your contract expires? What are the deconversion fees to get your data onto another core system?

We will cover the core contract in a little more added detail in Chapter 10 – The Golden Window.

CHAPTER 7

COST SAVINGS

L et's look at cost savings in more detail.

An acquisition that leaves all the personnel in place along with little to no operational changes still results in cost savings. It is important to recognize that there are still redundancies like two data processing contracts, two financial audits, two payroll systems, employee benefits duplication, and so forth.

The two core processing systems can be merged into one. The two financial audits can be performed by one of the two firms, not both. Employee benefit plans can be winnowed down to one - perhaps choosing between the two healthcare plan options, the same for dental plans, vision plans and life and disability insurance. One flexible spending plan will remain. So, even with all of the personnel left in place and with little to no changes operationally for the customers, a cost savings still results.

The average cost savings are 33%. This 33% does factor in some headcount reduction, primarily in duplicated back office roles.

In other words, the median transaction results in a 33% decrease in the seller's expenses.

The average seller may have an efficiency ratio of 70% before a deal and after the deal that drops to 47%.

Cost reductions create value.

Size creates scalability. Scalability creates higher earning power. But you may see that larger banks don't necessarily have better multiples than smaller banks. Again, you've got to be careful with multiples.

As banks get bigger, their efficiency gets better, and they make more money as a result. The earnings in the price to earnings ratio (P/E) increases. As the earnings (denominator) go up, the P/E ratio goes down. It goes down, not because they are worth less, but because the efficiency savings of a large bank are less than the efficiency savings for a community bank. If a larger bank was to sell, it would have less savings on a percentage basis to offer a buyer.

So, put another way, a target that is less efficient than the median may be added value to a buyer and the savvy seller will push this benefit during negotiations (another great reason to have a seasoned, productive sell-side investment banker alongside).

Here's some data, from my perspective, which shines some light on this:

Efficiency Ratio – Median of All U.S. Institutions by Size

Asset Size	Efficiency Ratio
< $250 million	70.4%
$250 - $500 million	64.0%
$500 million - $1 billion	62.8%
$1 - $3 billion	61.4%
$3 - $5 billion	56.6%
$5 - $10 billion	55.0%
> $10 billion	57.4%

* Financial data LTM as of March 31, 2022.   Source: S&P Global

As a smaller bank grows, people and technology are typically added in "chunks." You add people and technology to take care of the growth and to reduce risk. You then take a dip in profitability until that growth offsets the additional expense and subsequently, profitability grows to be more than the added expense. It stays that way for a period of time until, once again, additional growth causes added expense with the addition of more people and more technology. It is a repetitive process.

This chart says a great deal about what I have just described. If a bank five to seven times your total asset size is typically the buyer, then the buyer for a $225 million bank is approximately $1.1 billion - $1.6 billion. The efficiency ratio, on average, is going from 70.4% to 61.4%.

Let's stay with this example and breakdown the purchase further for demonstration.

Let's look at what the buyer is paying and the earnings the buyer is getting in exchange.

This is hypothetical. For example, the buyer has agreed to pay $30 million, at least that's what it says in the press release. What are they *actually* paying?

Here is the data the public doesn't see.

There might be transaction costs of $3 million. These are priced in and may include data processing costs (we will discuss this further in Chapter 10 – The "Golden Window"), Change-In-Control employee contract costs (we discuss this further in Chapter 9 – Talent), sign changes, short-term duplications in costs associated with employee benefits, audit firms, payroll providers and the like. Again, this is a hypothetical example but let's say this is all done for $3 million, in one-time costs.

There might be a $2 million credit adjustment (referred to as a "credit mark") following the due diligence loan review by the buyer. Consider it the provision they are adding as a cushion on the loan portfolio. Again, it is being assumed asset quality for the bank is good—this isn't a troubled bank that's being purchased.

Let's say there's a $2 million fixed asset/interest rate/ deposit mark as well.

Those adjustments total $7 million.

That means the announced price tag is $30 million, but it's a *net number* and what the seller's shareholders will receive, but the buyer is really paying $37 million and that is what they are concerned about.

Let's now look at the earnings the buyer is getting in exchange.

The seller is making a $2 million net profit on its own, but there's an additional $1 million in after-tax cost savings. This again is the *average* 33% savings (tax effected, so 50% estimated in after-tax cost savings).

The buyer is therefore getting $2 million, plus another $1 million, for a total of $3 million in earnings. They are unlocking, in this hypothetical example, 50% higher earnings. Maybe the scale and the scope will be higher or lower, but this is as straightforward an example as can be made.

This is the reason so many banks are looking at acquisitions. The combination of the two banks increases profitability.

The efficiency ratio data also seems to show that most banks are trying to grow to the $5 - $10 billion total asset size as the earnings are best in that size range, a 55% efficiency ratio, and $7 billion in total assets would seem to be a "sweet spot" in earnings. As the bank grows closer to $10 billion in total assets, some of that profit is lost to regulatory compliance costs building up to where they need to be for crossing over the $10 billion line.

With the efficiency ratio being 55% as an average for the $5 - $10 billion size, that would lead me to believe it's closer to 50% at around $7 billion in assets.

So, another way of putting it and to summarize the difference scale brings to the picture, it costs a bank below $250 million in total assets 70 cents to bring in $1 of revenue. It costs a $7 billion bank 50 cents to bring in $1 of revenue.

The increased regulatory burden when crossing over the $10 billion assets level makes the bank less profitable and is what moves the efficiency ratio higher. It costs that bank 57 cents to bring in $1 of revenue.

The cost savings outlined here represent hard dollar savings. Let's take a deeper look into strategic value that may be considered.

CHAPTER 8

STRATEGIC VALUE

W e touched on the beginning aspects of strategic value in Chapter 1 – Reverse Engineer, when we briefly went over the importance of finding both key similarities and differences between the acquiring bank and the bank being acquired. Finding the areas where the combination of two banks creates value greater than the sum of the parts can lead to higher deal value and increasing the buyer's willingness to pay a premium.

This chapter is meant to heighten your awareness level of strategic considerations, so you can think about those suggested below and add anything that may be specific to your bank. There are no right or wrong answers here. Beauty is in the eye of the beholder, but it is very important to be attuned to the possibilities.

We'll begin with the following possible strategic considerations to stimulate your thoughts:

- Does the target bank expand the acquirer's geographic footprint?
  - o If so, would the expanded footprint be in stronger or weaker markets?
    - Don't get caught up with stronger or weaker meaning "good" or "bad." To a fast-growing bank in a metropolitan market trying to fund the demand, a slower-growth market, which

could be viewed as "weaker" but is rich with longstanding, highly diversified deposits would potentially be a desirable trait.

- What types of customers will be acquired?

  o Retail/consumer, commercial, agricultural, residential builders, commercial real estate (investor property and/or owner occupied)?

  o At what cost?

    ▪ Will the costs be direct costs or indirect costs, such as the direct costs associated with adding additional support staff to ensure regulatory compliance, that would occur if you were adding a substantial number of retail customers? Indirect costs such as additional education if adding new lines of business such as agriculture lending or mortgage warehousing? What are the costs both initially and over time?

      • An acquirer who is in a market where residential building is growing, who doesn't have a residential construction function, may be able to gain the function in an acquisition to offset a planned expense in the future, saving that expense and lowering the cost of acquiring a residential construction portfolio going forward.

      • This could also lead to added mortgage lending fee income to an existing mortgage function or create the critical mass necessary to start one.

- Is there a significant branch/market overlap that could lead to substantial cost savings?

  o Or are the branch/markets of the two banks complementary, lowering the future costs of expanding the branch/market for the acquirer?

- Does the acquisition have the potential to enhance the overall franchise value?

  o Perhaps this is a larger bank with several locations throughout a region, but it is predominately in rural markets and the financial markets value the stock lower because the markets are slower growth. Perhaps an acquisition in a growing metropolitan area will be viewed by the financial markets as a positive whereas a lower loan-to-deposit bank, with lower cost deposits can deploy more loans and increase the earning power of the bank.

- Are the two cultures similar?

  o In the bullet just prior to this, it was considered that a bank with a large, predominantly rural market base acquired a metropolitan bank. This can be a strong combination under the right circumstances, but if the culture of the two banks is too different, it could cause the execution of the combination to go poorly and produce suboptimal results. We've seen banks from rural markets enter the Kansas City area over the years to deploy deposits from those markets into loans in the growing metro area. On paper, that looks like a great strategy. In reality, though, some of those banks didn't have any relationships developed in the market. Without having long-standing relationships in the market, credit standards can be lowered just due to lack of knowledge. Some of those banks loaned money to newly established home builders. In most cases, that didn't go well. The financial crisis of 2007 hit and some of the builders went out of business and those banks followed suit. That has since created hesitation, in my opinion, by other rural market banks from entering the market. I would argue that the entry into the market through an acquisition of an existing, proven bank, with long-standing customer relationships would have produced different results. That same thing could work in reverse as well. Some may consider the cultural differences are the reason the combination doesn't work, when in fact, it would appear to be an error in strategy.

- Will the acquisition diversify or enhance the acquirer's loan or deposit mix?

- Will the acquisition diversify or enhance fee income opportunities?

- Will the acquisition diversify or enhance the acquirer's balance sheet?

- Will the acquisition diversify or enhance the acquirer's technology offerings? Perhaps one of the two banks has an expertise in IT and the other may be a bit behind the times in their product offerings or internal efficiencies for fear of introducing cybersecurity risks.

- Will the acquisition diversify or enhance the acquirer's talent pool? We will discuss this further in Chapter 9 – Talent.

- Will the acquisition diversify or enhance the acquirer's succession plan?

- Will the acquisition diversify or enhance the acquirer's board? Will the boards bring new areas of expertise together like a board member with an IT background or a board member with a background in human resources.

- What other cost savings or revenue enhancements does this potential acquisition provide?

These are just a few thoughts to get ideas flowing. The strategic considerations are only limited by your imagination.

We'll focus next on talent-related strategic considerations.

CHAPTER 9

TALENT

Your job as the CEO is to make yourself replaceable. You do that by hiring the right people to keep the company going without you.

Don't get me wrong, you have unique and specialized talents like being a visionary, being adaptable, being a motivator, and being receptive as a listener. You have guided the bank toward success through skilled leadership and trusted decision-making. No matter how high and far you look, you won't find a leader who can do exactly what you do.

Prior to beginning the process of starting the bank, I was fortunate to have learned through my credit training and capital markets/corporate finance experience that if you're going to sell the bank (or any other business) at some point, a potential acquirer will want to see that you have a management team that can keep the bank running smoothly while you're gone.

The successful continuation of the profitable operation of the bank in your absence is critical to the overall value. This is true whether you are selling or not.

Your purpose as a leader does not lie in the tasks you spend your time on. Running a bank is full of strategic initiatives that can create long task lists that include everything from administrative duties to business development, and as CEO with these tasks on your plate, it's time to take a closer look at where you spend your time.

Your job as CEO is not to complete a to-do list—it's to make yourself replaceable.

Work **on** the business, not **in** it.

Systems, processes, and leadership are the keys to long-term value. And your people are the keys to systems, processes, and leadership.

Not a person in the singular sense but people as a group.

That's where the hard part comes in—shared values, attitudes, and beliefs—that's culture.

The CEO's primary responsibility is as the "Keeper of the Culture."

It isn't because the CEO is special. It is because the CEO's values, attitudes, and beliefs are going to be the ultimate decision-making criteria when an opportunity, issue, problem or complaint makes it to the CEO.

So, to have a strong culture and for your people to have long-term career satisfaction there needs to be shared values, attitudes, and beliefs.

The strong culture creates consistency.

Consistency is what customers look for. Not randomness. Not chaos.

Consistency.

Consistency is why McDonald's has sold billions of hamburgers despite never having won a cooking award. You know how that cheeseburger will taste in Washington

DC, Topeka, Tucson, New Orleans, Seattle, Pittsburgh, Boise, Boston, or Fargo.

Consistency as to how accounts get opened, how customers are on-boarded, how they are welcomed by name, how customers are listened to, how attentive your employees are to your customers, how quickly the phone gets answered, how accountable your people are to get the customer's issues resolved, even down to how well your employees are dressed. It is the consistency in business bankers going out to see the customers instead of making them come into the bank. It is consistency in everything. Is the grass green? Is the landscaping manicured? Is there trash blowing around in the parking lot? Is the flag tattered?

Every detail communicates that consistency. It all matters.

Accompanying the consistency in culture is the consistency in the systems, processes, and leadership.

When you have a culture of consistency, you're going to see a rising benefit in your bank. Customers are telling everybody about your bank and your employees are happy in their careers, looking forward to what they can <u>do</u> and <u>become</u> (common theme here).

Getting to this point is rarified air, but it should be the goal.

Achievement of the goal is extremely difficult.

If the CEO doesn't diligently play the role of "Keeper of the Culture," it can be gone overnight.

That's the role the CEO needs to be playing. In addition to this role, the CEO's role is to look three to five years ahead to see where the company can build the most value.

If a CEO is actively involved in customer relationships on a day-to-day basis or is somehow involved in the day-to-day grind of the business, so much so that the CEO becomes a bottleneck for the business, talent will likely be a value detractor for an acquirer. The interaction you will have with prospective buyers throughout the process of selling will provide the insight they are looking for. How often during the time you spend with potential buyers do you have to take calls from the bank answering questions for your people? How hard is it to get your time because you have things that must get done first? When your people are being interviewed by potential buyers how much do they look to you to answer questions (see Chapter 23 – Management Meetings)? These are all indicators that <u>you</u> *are the business*. That may be kind to your ego, but it will detract from the bank's overall value.

You might still be able to sell, but your bargaining power will suffer and the number of potentially interested parties will get smaller.

If you've got a great culture and rock-solid systems, processes, and procedures already in place and you are not involved in the day-to-day function of the bank. Great job!

If you aren't in a position where you are not involved in the day-to-day function of the bank, I get it. I've been there. It's hard to let go and allow other people to take control.

But it doesn't have to be that way.

Now having said all of that, I'm just going to lay it on the line for you.

Your buyer isn't going to care about your culture.

And please understand what I am saying here. Your culture is vital to your bank. It is vital to the success you have had and it's why your customers love your bank.

But the buyer has their own CEO and therefore, they have their own culture. Talking about your culture during your first meeting (we will be discussing further in Chapter 17 – One-On-One Meetings) with them will be entirely proper—they will need the context. Beyond that, drop your expectation that your culture will survive. It won't. Unless it is a unique circumstance, it *shouldn't*. It is possible that the values, attitudes, and beliefs of the two CEOs are a dead match – if that is the case, that's awesome. It's just not very likely.

What they will be looking for is a bank that has rock-solid systems, processes, and procedures and the people in place to continue to drive the earnings. Again, it's steady, predictable, and consistent earnings that hold their interest. Their future depends on those earnings.

They will be very interested in making certain that those key people will be coming along with a high level of interest in being a part of their bank and will want to be there for a long time. Again, they are thinking "Do & Become." The more they can project that into the future of the bank, the more interested they are.

I won't sugarcoat it. The people they will be most interested in are those who are directly tied to customer relationships—calling officers, retail personnel, and customer service teams. They are also interested in senior level team members who can help with the transition and make that go as smoothly as possible.

In today's day and age, it should be that the buyer would want to keep everybody they possibly can because they likely have needs throughout their bank to be filled. But pay scale differences of different markets and perhaps, just an embedded belief that they don't need to do anything other than what they've historically done to fill those roles may have them viewing things differently. A bank with a mostly rural presence entering a metropolitan market may be in for a shock when they compare the cost differences of people in the different markets. Conversely, a major metro area bank may look to expand the team in a rural market to provide additional jobs for that market while taking advantage of a potentially lower cost of living in that market.

Enough said about that. Let's get back to you!

Culture is vitally important, and your people are critical to the successful delivery of that culture. Your customers love your bank because of your culture and your people.

Your overall goal here is to provide value the shareholders will be pleased with. You should be looking for ways to move to a bigger platform your employees can excel in so they can extend their careers. And to add more borrowing capacity, products, and platforms for your customers to continue to succeed. Achieving those goals will bring continued value to your community.

You have perhaps kissed more than your fair share of toads along the way looking for the right people. I know we did. It takes a great deal of energy to get the right people on board the bus and that often means making sure the wrong people are off the bus. It's very hard work. But it too is the consistency that comes with shared values, attitudes, and beliefs of the right people on the bus. People can say they have shared values, attitudes, and beliefs to get on the bus, but if they truly don't, the lack of those shared values, attitudes, and beliefs will show up in their lack of consistency with the details.

The team you found, recruited, hired, and developed, and have put your blood, sweat and tears into so they can run the bank without you is very dear to you. You want them to be able to take part in the value they have helped to create. You offered them the opportunity to buy stock when it became available. Those who could take advantage of that did. Others might have been unable to do that because of their financial circumstances at the time the stock was available. Or perhaps there wasn't any stock available to offer as shareholders held onto their stock.

The people who are responsible, *and most importantly are accountable*, for the various functions of the bank are people you are going to likely want to protect. You have trained and developed them. The last thing you want is to be the training department for a competitor with them just throwing money at their problems instead of doing the hard work necessary to build their own team.

The way to protect them is through Change-In-Control (CIC) agreements, and you will want to strongly consider Stay-Put features as well. This includes you, the CEO. A CIC provides a lump sum payment to you to diminish the inevitable distraction and personal uncertainties and risks that are created by a potential change in control. It allows key employees to know they will have a financial incentive if it were to happen so they can forget about it and focus on their role. A Stay-Put agreement also assures the key employees they have continued employment with the new owner or if the new owner decides they are not needed, will pay the key employee another lump sum payment at the time the Stay-Put feature expires (typically 12 months) or whenever the new owner feels they are no longer needed, whichever comes first. This should be something the board should want to strongly get behind as well because it is in the best interests of the shareholders.

Reasons you may hear for not having CIC's and Stay-Puts could be that it is a lot of money. You may hear, "Who's going to pay for this?" Or "Won't the buyers balk at that? Won't they want to decide who stays and who goes?"

Who pays for it can be a matter of opinion. It likely will be factored into the value of the bank and subtracted from the value to ultimately end in the share price the shareholders will receive. But I would argue that it will create more value in the gross number before it is netted out. So, you tell me; Who pays for it?

What would happen to your value after you have found, recruited, hired, and developed key talent who left right before you were going to begin looking for a buyer, or if you were already early in the process? You are protecting your shareholders' value by putting these agreements in place. You are also rewarding those key employees for the value they are helping to create.

The buyer will want to ensure that the people critical to producing the ongoing future profits of the business stay with the bank. The Stay-Put feature does not guarantee future employment beyond the terms of the agreement. What it does do is eliminate the need to put these in place as a contingency to closing the deal at a time when the leverage would dramatically shift to the key employees and could impact the whole deal getting done. The employees ultimately are on-boarded to the buyer when the deal closes with a renewed enthusiasm for what the future holds rather than immediately entertaining offers from the competition.

It does need to be said that CICs should be *considered* for people you know you want for the long haul and who understand and contribute to the culture. <u>This should not be a tool handed out as a recruiting "sweetener."</u> It is something that should be used *very sparingly* for those critical to carrying out the day-to-day function of the bank. The people who should be covered by CICs are those people who can carry on all the functions of the bank, and do it daily, *so that you're not needed*. That ultimately makes a more valuable bank.

That is what most buyers are looking for.

But again, you will have a CIC as well, with Stay-Put provisions as well. So, if you are needed, you are available, and if you aren't needed, you have been compensated for your willingness to have stuck around. Fully understand you are likely working yourself out of a job (and I am assuming you are on the board when I say this). But it is your fiduciary duty to maximize shareholder value *ahead of* your personal interest of employment.

So, again, what are CICs and what do they look like? *Keep in mind, I am not a lawyer, so it is strongly recommended that you seek legal counsel on your CICs.*

A CIC is an offering to an employee, in addition to the salary they are making. It's generally a lump sum payment of a multiple of their salary should a sale of the controlling interest in the bank's stock be sold. A lump sum payment equaling that multiple would be paid to them, within 30 days of the change in control.

In addition to that, the employee would be paid another multiple of their salary if they stay for a prescribed period of time following the change in control (typically one year). Again, with a lump sum due to them within 30 days of passing that date.

In exchange for that, the employee agrees to certain things such as confidentiality, and non-solicitation of employees and customers for a period of typically 12 months following their termination of employment.

There are IRS 280-G requirements that do need to be taken into consideration—essentially how much the combined payments (CIC and Stay-Put) total in comparison to the employee's base salary—and the attorney and your accountant can aid in guiding you there.

In general, the two payments can total up to $2 - 3$ times total compensation. This is a standard rule of thumb.

This is something that would require board approval, and the regulators will want to review as well during their exams.

This shortens the conversation with the buyer about the risk of people, which are critical to the function of the bank, leaving when the deal is announced or in the middle of the stream. It also aids in protecting your other employees and customers to a degree through the non-solicitation features.

I can say with certainty the competition will be doing everything they can to get in front of your employees as soon as the deal is announced. Your employees can move on without the distraction of those calls because they have a fair amount of money on the line, and they will likely want to see what the opportunity looks like with the buyer.

When is the best time to actively consider selling?

We'll talk about that in the next chapter.

CHAPTER 10

THE GOLDEN WINDOW

I f you could pick a time that presents the "best" time to begin the process of looking for a buyer, what would you base it on? I would base it on the moment when your safety & soundness, BSA and IT exams have just successfully completed, and you have 18 months until the next exam cycle (realizing that compliance and CRA exams are on different schedules), AND your core contract is 18-24 months from completion as well.

This is what I refer to as "The Golden Window."

I call it that for three reasons. The first is because you have just completed an exam and don't have that distraction while the process is taking place. The second is you have just gone through the information request for the exam so there won't be the need for a suspicious information request associated with the process (maybe a few additions, but not a wholesale request). And third, the most important reason, your core contract will likely have the least negative impact on the price your shareholders would realize in the sale.

Your core contract has two major impacts on the price. The first is the *early termination fee*. The fee you likely must pay to end your contract. You will want to affirm your contract end date with your core provider, and you'll want to do this as inconspicuously as possible so as not to alert your team or the core provider to the possibility of a sale. This could be built in as a part of your annual review of your vendor management program.

Your vendor management program provides a review of all third-party contracts for your board, covering:

- A summary on risk management related to the third-party vendor.

- Who is affected by the risk associated with the vendor—your customers, your operations, etc.

- Issues to be considered relative to the risk—the impact and severity of the risk.

- Reporting requirements associated with the level of risk, external audit reports, etc.

Along with these things, include building a termination and exit strategies section for each third-party contract as part of your annual review. Review if there are any early termination fees and how those fees will be handled, identified by the vendor, as well as the notification process for each vendor. This is very important information for you to have available whenever you need it.

The early termination fee is essentially your "make-whole" to the core provider for the remaining term on your contract. Say you just entered a seven-year core contract so you can get the best monthly pricing. You then later decide to sell and have 54 months left on your core contract when the closing date is scheduled to take place. You will be liable for 80% of your contracted payments (a ballpark estimate and your contract may vary) through the remainder of the contract. You may also need to add back credits you received as inducements when you entered into the contract if you end the contract early.

That can be a staggering number and completely change the complexion of whether you (or likely the shareholders) would want to move forward with a sale.

Let's look at two hypothetical scenarios. This example is for a community bank with $200 million in assets. You will have to do your own analysis of your contract for the actual impact. This is for illustration purposes only.

The first scenario is with 54 months remaining when the sale closes, and the second scenario is identical to the first, with the only difference being 12 months remaining when the sale closes.

Scenario #1 – 54 months remaining (For those listening to the audiobook please go to www.KurtKnutson.com/BonusContent for the worksheet referenced here):

Average Monthly Cost	Months Remaining	Percentage	Total
$30,500	54	80%	$1,317,600

Monthly Credits			
$2,870	54	100%	$154,980
		TOTAL	$1,472,580

Scenario #2 – 12 months remaining (For those listening to the audiobook please go to www.KurtKnutson.com/ BonusContent for the worksheet referenced here):

Average Monthly Cost	Months Remaining	Percentage	Total
$30,500	12	80%	$292,800

Monthly Credits			
$2,870	12	100%	$34,440
		TOTAL	**$327,240**

The closer the closing date can be to the contract expiration the better. That's why I refer to the time as "The Golden Window" because it is a short, often fleeting period during which a rare and desired action can be taken and because of the amount of money that could be saved. It's easier said than done. If you can strategically build it into your process, the better off you'll be. The core contract expiration needs to be factored in for sure.

Again, I would suggest you consider bringing your core contract and all the ancillary addendums to your board for review once a year as a matter of standard practice as a part of your vendor management program. By focusing on it during the annual board schedule, it becomes a regular item, taking the unusual one-off review out of the equation. Now I know that it is likely included in your vendor management review now, but I emphasize that focus should be heightened to include the early termination fee as a part of the annual review—the actual number. It will cause the team to put it on a schedule for the board's review where all the ancillary addendums, like mobile banking, account analysis, treasury services, imaging, etc., will be brought to the forefront and your team will need to review and stay current with any changes that may extend your core contract in a "hidden" way. The board's persistent attention to this will likely make your team more aware and accountable.

The review will cause the team to tie everything back together to an agreed upon contract termination date. The *board should get affirmation from the team by specifically asking for confirmation of exactly when the termination date is.* The practice will make for better contract negotiation as well, because it will focus your team on the importance of that date and the possibility of leveraging the date in future negotiations. It can easily be explained to your team, from an educational perspective, that contracts carrying termination fees can have a significant impact on the future cash flow of the bank which can therefore impact the value of the bank.

The second impact on the price is the *deconversion fee*. The deconversion fee, is the charge you will incur for moving your data to the new system, has an impact on your sales price as well. Knowing this and focusing on it once a year in front of the board also keeps it front of mind for negotiation as well. Leveraging the possible removal of the deconversion fees with the core provider when considering new products or extensions should be a high priority. If the deconversion fees can't be negotiated away, perhaps a fallback could be for the calculation of the fee to be fully and clearly defined. Without the definition of the calculation, the leverage shifts dramatically in favor of the core provider who can name their price.

Another example could be your debit card processing contract.

Like the process of taking your core contract annually, consider taking all contracts over a certain value (like $25,000) in front of your board once a year. This may sound frivolous, but, if you are in a situation where you sell the bank you will likely need to produce these during your due diligence for your definitive agreement (often referred to as the merger agreement interchangeably, we will refer to it throughout this book as the definitive agreement). Again, if they become a standard agenda item for review annually, there is no unusual nature to the production of the results. There is a higher valued placed on these items by your team since there is board scrutiny and the review and production of accompanying documents is never more than twelve months old.

You may have the Golden Window approaching soon, so in the next chapter we'll consider the shareholders and their desires.

CHAPTER 11

SHAREHOLDERS

A s a bank CEO you are familiar with acting as a fiduciary. We all can become "house blind" to the specifics of those duties. Refreshers of the fiduciary duties of good faith, care and loyalty are helpful periodically, and especially when considering the sale of the bank. As with any corporate decision, the directors should ensure that they are informed and knowledgeable of the material aspects of the transaction.

The primary responsibility of the board of directors, as fiduciaries, is to maximize value to the shareholders.

The fiduciary duties of the board of directors and corporate officers are unique to the laws of each state. As a reminder, the information in this book is not intended to be a substitute for legal advice or legal counsel. Generally, the officers, directors, and controlling shareholders are bound to the fiduciary duties of <u>good faith</u>, <u>care</u>, and <u>loyalty</u>.

The duty of **good faith** focuses on the <u>motivation</u> in making a certain corporate decision. *When acting in good faith, the primary motive is to advance the best interests of the corporation and the shareholders.* Errors in judgment are generally not enough to establish one acted in bad faith. Bad faith is typically inferred only where the corporate decision is so far beyond the bounds of reasonable judgment that the decision is inexplicable on any other ground other than bad faith. Making a decision to approve a loan that eventually goes bad could have elements of bad judgment if a thorough analysis demonstrated it was a risky bet the bank would be repaid. Deciding to approve a loan with a high likelihood the bank wouldn't be repaid because you were afraid to say no is an example of operating in bad faith.

The duty of **care** requires the <u>exercise of a degree of skill, diligence, and care</u> that a reasonably prudent person would exercise when acting in the best interests of the corporation and shareholders. *To fulfill the duty of care, all material facts related to a proposed act or transaction and all information available should be considered before acting.* Directors should also play an active role in the decision-making process by making reasonable inquiries into the proposed act or transaction.

In fulfilling their duty of care, directors are entitled to rely in good faith on the records of the corporation and any information, opinions, reports, or statements presented to the board by officers, employees, committees, or by any other person the board believes are within their professional or expert competence.

The duty of **loyalty** requires directors to <u>not act primarily for personal or non-corporate purposes</u>. For example, corporate acts or decisions motivated by a director's desire to preserve their position, compensation, or prerequisites at the expense of the corporation or its shareholders. *The duty of loyalty prevents directors from engaging in "self-dealing" transactions to gain improper benefit—financial or otherwise—from the transaction.*

The board may want to contemplate the following actions when considering and approving the sale of the bank:

- Obtain a "fairness opinion." A fairness opinion is a document provided by the seller's investment banker to the seller's board of directors attesting to the fairness of a transaction from a financial point of view. The purpose of the fairness opinion is to provide selling shareholders with an objective third-party analysis of the deal's fairness. The fairness opinion is designed to protect the shareholders from situations where management and shareholders' interests are not aligned. Management may favor one bidder over another, for example, because the terms of the employment post-acquisition were more favorable. The fairness opinion is designed to protect shareholders from these types of situations while also protecting seller management teams and boards from shareholder lawsuits upon consummation of the deal.

- Consider alternatives to the sale of the bank and the possible ranges of those alternatives. The alternatives are growing the bank organically, buying another bank, selling the bank, or merging with a like-sized bank often referred to as a "merger of equals."

- Assess the market to find the likelihood of obtaining a higher price from another potential purchaser.

- Ensure the transaction documents allow for a "fiduciary out" and consider whether the transaction documents allow for adequate deal certainty. There are three common forms of fiduciary outs:

  o A right for the board to consider superior third-party offers and accept one to replace the current, signed agreement. This is the most common, and unobjectionable fiduciary out.

o A right for the board to change its recommendation and end the agreement because of an intervening event, unknown to the directors at signing, which causes the bank to become substantially worth more than its valuation at signing.

o A general right of the board to change its recommendation and end the agreement because of a good faith finding, on the advice of counsel, that not doing so would violate the board's fiduciary duties. In the absence of a specific reason like a superior offer or intervening event, this fiduciary out is the least common.

- Consider the acquirer's past performances of financial obligations and the ability of the potential acquirer to finance its offer and obtain regulatory approval.

- Maintain an active role in the oversight of the sale process. The board's oversight should be independent from the bank's management.

- Disclose any conflicts of interest to the board and to the shareholders of the bank. Here again is an example where bank management's goals and the shareholder goals may be out of alignment. One offer may hold big things for the management team: big salaries and big roles, but the offer price may be lower than another offer. This, in and of itself, may not be enough to choose one over the other. However, it should be fully disclosed so that it can be factored into the decision-making process.

- Maintain a complete written record of the above-mentioned actions and any other actions taken by the board.

The processes recommended do not guarantee that a board's decision will not be challenged or guarantee that a court would find that a board fulfilled its duties; however, including these actions in the sale process can significantly ensure that the process was conducted in good faith and on an informed basis.

Here are a series of questions to aid in stimulating thought around any issues related to shareholders. *This is by no means an exhaustive list of considerations*. Each situation is uniquely related to shareholders. The idea here is to try to bring to light anything you may need to navigate or can possibly mitigate prior to the sale process and up to and including the closing.

What does your current shareholder mix look like?

Does your shareholder mix have high concentrations of ownership?

Does your shareholder mix have a family or families with significant concentrations of ownership?

If so, are they removed from the founding of the bank and are no longer active in it, or are they still actively involved aside from the ownership interest?

Are your shares more widely distributed with no one person owning more than 10%?

Do you have patient capital, or is there a need for liquidity amongst your shareholders?

Would your shareholders be interested in exchanging their stock for that of a buyer or would your shareholders be interested in cash?

Do you have any stock options or stock warrants currently outstanding?

Are there any share transfers in process or expected to take place soon?

Have you revisited your corporate documents recently, and/or have you had outside counsel revisit them (e.g., shareholders agreement, articles, by-laws, etc.)? Is everything in order and current?

Are there any considerations you need to be aware of surrounding a sale that require advanced planning?

Have you had an independent valuation of the stock recently? If so, was it distributed to all shareholders? Was the valuation for a minority interest?

Are your shareholder records current?

What reaction are you most fearful of coming from your shareholders about a sale?

Did the most recent annual meeting go well? Were there any issues that were brought up at the annual meeting that are not resolved? How was attendance, both in-person and by proxy? Was the attendance—in-person or by proxy—higher or lower than the previous year's trend? Was the mix—in-person or by proxy—trending one way or another or staying the same?

The fiduciary duties listed at the beginning of this chapter should provide guidance, or the framework, for dealing with most shareholder issues and concerns.

Shareholder considerations are varied and can be very complicated. If the board acts in accordance with their fiduciary duties, it goes a long way to mitigating risk within the shareholder base.

Let's look at considerations for putting together your advisory team in the next chapter.

CHAPTER 12

BUILDING AN ADVISOR TEAM

When you bring serious people to the table, you are signaling to your potential buyer pool, "We are serious." Your advisor team are the serious people you are bringing to the table. Your investment banker, your lawyer, and your accountant.

When you're thinking about the lifespan of the bank, to use a baseball game as a metaphor, the best time to sell is in the fifth or sixth inning. At this point, you have put a bunch of runs on the scoreboard, you've got the lead and you have the heart of the lineup coming up. Basically, you have control over the game. You're projecting victory, you're projecting wins. I say that because buyers are buying future cash flows and your future looks bright.

When you're starting to slow down, your growth rate is starting to slow, you're not going to get the same valuations. If you start losing money or the competition is starting to step on you, it's more difficult to sell, and certainly valuation comes down.

Sellers generally fall into one of three buckets or some combination of the buckets.

The *first bucket* is called "**Inbound Interest**" and is made up of sellers who contact investment bankers well in advance of a sale. They are getting smart about M&A before they're thrown into the deep end of the pool.

The *second bucket* is called the **"Turning Point"** and is made up of sellers who have reached some point of inflection where they have done a calculation and there is an impending industry downturn on the horizon, and they don't want to go through a drop in value and several years of returning to the industry valuation they are at today. Another reason could be a substantial investment upcoming (which may or may not require additional capital but will certainly dampen earnings in the short run) that needs to be made which will reduce the value in the short term and will eventually increase the value, but they don't want to go through the time and risk to get there.

The *third bucket* is called **"Succession"** and is made up of seeing retirement on the horizon or a partner with a health issue, and they don't want to go through the process of finding, recruiting, hiring, and/or developing the talent needed for their replacement. In this example, perhaps the one or two key people with the bank have not done a good job finding, recruiting, hiring, and developing talent (as pointed out in Chapter 9 – Talent) and have not made themselves "replaceable." Now, one of the two of them has a major health issue and the other is looking at the daunting task realizing that this illness may interfere with his or her own exit of the business and therefore wants to sell to transfer that duty to the buyer (knowingly or unknowingly, depending on the effectiveness of due diligence).

For those who may be thinking, "I don't want to scare somebody away by involving an investment banker right out of the gate," I can promise you that a serious buyer would love to see somebody involved who understands the M&A process.

Knowing that your value may go up a bit by using an investment banker is a trade-off they will gladly take because a serious investment banker increases the percentages that the deal will get done. So, to them, success is about cutting friction and mitigating risk throughout the process to maximize the probability of making the acquisition succeed in the long term, not saving a couple of bucks on the front end.

The right investment banker immediately introduces to the buyer on one phone call that the seller is serious about selling and that the investment banker can create competition for this opportunity. The buyer knows if this call doesn't go well, the investment banker has a list of potentially interested buyers to call next. This is a critical point because with an investment banker, you take control of the process; without an investment banker representing you, the buyer has control.

This all helps you maximize value and keeps everything on a timeline. Our investment banker, Christopher Olsen of Olsen Palmer, often reminded us "You never step in the same river twice," borrowed from the ancient Greek philosopher Heraclitus' quote: "No man ever steps in the same river twice, for it is not the same river and he is not the same man." Time represents risk, and as bankers, we know that very well—our business is based upon it.

The work you have been doing in the prior chapters is all to help prepare you for conversations with your investment banker. They will need to be fully prepared to know all the warts and red flags because the buyer will see them, and your investment banker will want to have enough knowledge, so they aren't taken off guard. The more they understand, the more they can match that against the landscape of potential buyers to find the best opportunities for you.

A sell-side investment banker in the bank M&A space is where you want to look for help. You may feel comfortable with somebody that does both buy-side and sell-side work, but my experience had me looking for *sell-side only* for this reason, and I am going to tell a personal story here to illustrate the point.

As a commercial banker, I specialized in the printing industry for six years. The bank I was working for at the time had banked great local printing companies who had been suppliers to Kansas City headquartered Hallmark Cards. The bank liked the industry because it was capital intensive, labor intensive and material intensive all requiring working capital and cash management services, and the collateral held its value extremely well on the term loan side of things. They wanted to find more good printing companies to loan money to in the surrounding states of Iowa, Kansas, Nebraska, and Missouri.

I knew nothing about the industry, but I enthusiastically jumped on the role and became a member of all the printing industry trade associations. I subscribed to all the industry's trade publications. That involvement took me to trade shows and conferences. I was typically the only banker in the crowd. That earned respect from the owners of the best printing companies in the country. They took an interest in me, and I took one in them. We became friends. Over the six years of calling, the territory expanded to include the entire continental United States.

My career took another turn when one of the largest banks in the country bought the bank that I was working for. The acquisition created an opportunity for me to gain a whole new set of additional skills. Those skills would later play an important role for me as it set me on a path for starting my own bank. Shortly after they bought the bank, they bought a well-known investment bank. Their strategy was to build a team of bankers who could sell the entire right side of the balance sheet: debt and equity. I was trained in capital markets and corporate finance so that I could find opportunities in which we could bring in investment bankers to complement what we were doing on the bank side of the house.

After a couple of years of doing that, a regional bank hired me to set up and build a capital markets/corporate finance group for them. The bank didn't have a captive investment bank, so I needed to develop relationships with multiple providers for each product along the capital markets spectrum. The prior training I received really gave me the foundation to be able to visualize putting this together and have conversations with all of the financial services providers needed to build out the practice. It allowed me to experience starting a business within an existing business, lessening the risk to me from financial loss personally. But it also gave me the experience of what it was like to start a business from scratch. From factoring to asset-based working capital, asset-based equipment finance, private placements of senior debt, commercial real estate private placements, mezzanine finance and equity, along with buy-side and sell-side M&A. Our group did everything the bank didn't do, so we could protect existing clients from being taken over by larger competitors and to be utilized as a lead in a relationship with our large competitors' customers.

I dealt with all sorts of investment bankers from all over the country and soon learned that they eat what they kill, meaning if they don't do deals, they don't get paid. They have lumpy (but large) cash flow, and they are generally adrenaline junkies, often working 60-80+ hours a week. I found the experience to be exhilarating, although from a different angle. I didn't have the same risk profile they had overall, but I did have commissions tied to the success (paid by the customer, not the provider). This also gave me the perspective of what starting my own business would be like, but again, without all the risk. It contributed to my ability to start a bank years later. I learned, like commercial bankers, there were relationship bankers and transaction bankers. The relationship bankers took the time to learn the backstory so they could draw upon the many resources embedded in those stories as potential to enhance the opportunity they were working on. Transactional bankers, on the other hand, didn't go the extra mile—they felt that was a waste of their time—and they didn't have time to waste. They needed to dedicate the most time they possibly could to opportunities that paid the bills. Focusing perhaps a bit more on quantity than maximizing fee potential on fewer deals.

To better illustrate where the difference in bankers can be, here's an example of what I am talking about. I was contacted by a fifth-generation printing company owner in the northeast United States. He said the family was trying to decide if they should sell one of their printing companies. The family had hired an investment banking group that was a subsidiary of a big four accounting firm to market the company. The family trusted the "name brand" to do a good job with the project. The gentleman I spoke with knew of my industry background and wanted to see if there was any way I could work with the investment bankers they had hired to increase the odds of success and maximize shareholder value. He asked me to contact the investment bankers as he had already had a conversation with them about it and they would be expecting my call. My insertion into this process was highly unusual.

When I called, it was obvious that the investment bankers didn't understand what, if any value, I could possibly bring to the table. After all they were a part of this well-known firm, they were based in Boston, and I was just some unknown banker at an unknown bank in the middle of fly-over country. Following my conversation with the bankers I connected with my contact again and said, I would be happy to work on the project for them, but it was apparent to me that I would need to have my own agreement with the family, separate and apart from the other bankers.

It was decided that we would each send a list of potentially interested parties, and if there was an overlap, the family would decide who would work with who and what course of action to take from there. Luckily, following the submission of our respective lists, we had no overlap. The Boston bankers sent a list of 25 parties, and I submitted a list of 10. No overlap. The reason there was no overlap was that the Boston bankers essentially put a coffee can on a map and drew a circle around the printing company and claimed all printing companies within the geographic area as theirs.

I, on the other hand, knew that this printing company specialized in printing seed packets—the types of seed packets you'd see hanging from a rack in the nursery, or the nursery section of the hardware store. I knew of the other printing companies in the country that were in the same niche. They had the equipment, processes, and sales team in place to make the acquisition take off immediately. As opposed to a general commercial printing company having to learn the business, the equipment set-up and having to introduce themselves to the seed producers.

We were both instructed to send out our "deal sheets" or "teasers" which is a summary of the opportunity without naming the company. I heard back from seven of my ten (70%) saying they wanted to take the next step of signing non-disclosure agreements (NDAs). The Boston investment bankers called about two weeks later asking how things were going and suddenly had a friendly tone. They didn't have any of the 25 prospects (0%) wanting to move on to the next step.

The point of the whole story is this: All investment bankers are not the same. Interview investment bankers the same way you would interview anybody else.

Yes, they may speak a different language, go at a different pace, and may be from another part of the country. But you only sell once. For my money, I would recommend looking for somebody whose sole focus is on bank M&A, and *primarily in sell-side bank M&A.*

Whether it is reducing risk on the transaction or on the price, a good investment banker can pay for themselves. A good sell-side investment banker helps with intelligence on potential buyers. They know who those buyers are talking to, or not talking to.

Your investment bankers are running the data room, negotiating, answering questions, swapping information, arranging meetings, coordinating schedules, and managing the project overall. Look for a high-touch, private client approach that includes a significant investment in getting to know your bank, helping relationship-building with potential buyers and being 24/7 advisors shepherding the deal all the way to the

Letter of Intent (LOI) and through closing, regardless of the size of your bank.

Preferably the firm you choose will have a broad reach to buyers throughout the United States, along with the sell-side expertise to analyze the offers and experience to avoid potential pitfalls. In short, look for sell-side specialization, which provides a lack of buyer conflicts.

It's an important decision to make, and investment bankers that understand the whole picture are likely to do a better job maximizing shareholder value on your deal than somebody who is just looking to do a deal.

Look beneath the surface. Build relationships with investment bankers. Attend their conferences and webinars. Meet with them at your state bank association conferences—they are often sponsors. Meet with them whenever possible for lunch, dinner, or drinks. Make note of who comes to see you while understanding their time is extremely valuable. Go out of your way to get to know them. In the end, with all else being equal, you will want to work with somebody you feel the most comfortable with.

In terms of legal counsel for your transaction, after having gone through the process, I can say with confidence you will want to collaborate with a firm who has a significant amount of experience in bank M&A. We will get into the process in Section 3 with a very particular focus on the legal counsel aspect in Chapter 28 – Definitive Agreement & Disclosure Schedules.

This is a very complex process with a great deal of moving parts. You also have a bank to run while assembling, navigating, and negotiating this part of the process. A significant portion of which is being done when nobody besides the board and small deal team knows you are even working on it.

An experienced legal team will keep you focused on the few sections you really need to pay attention to while working behind the scenes on the sections that you don't need to be involved with. They have so much repetition with the process that they will only pull you in when they run into something outside of the norm. Things like fees that are normally taken on by the buyer, information requests that are well beyond anything they have seen prior, and places where you can push back on these things because they have seen it work in some cases, but not in others. That familiarity with the process was very valuable. An experienced buyer, who was one of the potentially interested parties we had a one-on-one meeting with pulled me aside following our meeting and asked about who we were going to be using for deal counsel. His advice was to get somebody with experience for the reasons I just noted above. And in hindsight, I can say he was correct. Your defenses are up whenever somebody on the other side of a transaction is giving you advice. In this case, it was so early in the process that I didn't feel like I was being "worked" for an advantage. The message, after some time for reflection, really seemed wise and having been through the process, was genuine advice. You will want to consider using legal counsel with a great deal of *sell-side bank M&A experience* so it can allow you to focus on running the bank.

On the accounting side, we had fully audited statements. We had to have audited financials as a de novo bank for the first three years of our existence. We continued to get audited financial statements beyond that first requirement. That was a choice we made because we had about 80 investors (this number is provided for perspective, the number of shareholders for banks is all over the board) and we wanted to provide a level of comfort for our investors. Many banks our size or smaller don't have audited financial statements because of the annual cost. We didn't have any shareholders specifically requesting audited financials, but I know, as an investor, I would feel more comfortable knowing there are audited financials. Many of our investors were my family and friends and I didn't want anything to be awkward going forward so we went the extra mile. If you are considering a transaction soon, you may wish to consider getting audited financials. It may save you time and effort during the process if it is done beforehand. There will be testing that will need to take place and that can be much lighter if you already have it in-hand.

This is a complex process with moving parts, and you must get it right. This is not something you want to do for yourself. The right team of advisors will help you maximize the value, keep it on a timeline, and get the best results.

Section 1 is now complete. You are building a foundation for the process and gaining a great deal of perspective now on an understanding of what you're worth, when the right time to go to market may be, the board's responsibilities to the shareholders, and building an advisory team.

In Section 2, we will be focusing on whether there is any interest in the bank and the process of going to market to find out.

SECTION 2

WHO WANTS US?

CHAPTER 13

BOARD/ADVISORS/ INSIDER AGREEMENTS

I n the six or seven years leading up to the board's decision to explore whether we would be of a buyer's interest, we invited an investment banker to speak as our guest speaker during our annual meeting. This was something that was instilled in me when I was doing the capital markets/corporate finance work earlier in my career and prior to starting the bank. The importance of having investment bankers familiar with us, and us with them, would be a strength if we ever needed to engage their services. Better "to dig our well before we're thirsty" from my perspective. Each year we would feature an investment banker to review the state of the industry from an M&A perspective. We opted to hear from different investment bankers through the years. Hearing from different bankers provided different perspectives, although on the same topic. It was a great opportunity for our board to become familiar with the investment bankers, for the investment bankers to become more familiar with who we were and provided a great opportunity for our board, our management team, and our shareholders to understand the factors driving value, both from a macro and a micro perspective. Most investment bankers will make a presentation to your board for just the expenses associated with making a trip. They too enjoy the opportunity to meet the board.

The annual meeting presentation along with the annual review of our capital plan provided opportunities to educate the board and keep them updated on:

- Value drivers and detractors: ensuring our board understands what drives shareholder value as well as understanding it is not about multiples it is more about what a buyer's ability and willingness to pay.

- The sales process and timing: the key steps of a sale transaction, as well as the timing for each part of the process.

- Key deal terms: such as consideration type (all cash, cash & stock mix, all stock), the fixed exchange ratio (the relative number of shares given to an existing shareholder), severance and treatment of Change-In-Control contracts, contingent deal values and minimum equity covenants.

- Confidentiality: the importance of it in protecting value, employees, and customers.

- Role and value of an investment banker: ensuring the board understood the value and benefits such as superior pricing, market intelligence and awareness of buyers' deal appetites, the reduction of execution risk, and the freeing up of management so the bank would be successfully running during the process.

- Market timing: like the industry and economic conditions overall, bank M&A is cyclical, so it is important for the board to understand valuations and deal activity during the stages of the cycles.

These presentations over the years provided the educational backdrop for the presentation to the board and discussion about exploring the potential sale of the bank. As you can imagine, this was a very significant discussion! Despite making the decision to move forward to explore the market, we had no guarantee that we would find:

- A market that would be in our favor.

- Market conditions would hold favorable throughout the process.

- We would achieve a valuation that was attractive to the shareholders.

- We would find a good cultural fit for our employees.

- A strong match for our customer base that would provide more opportunity for our customers to grow with the surviving bank.

- All of this would remain highly confidential.

This was a highly uncertain process we were about to embark on.

To meet the significance of the occasion, we opted for a confidential special meeting of the board, off-site in a meeting room of a nearby hotel. The topic of anything other than organic growth or buying a bank, in my opinion, could be very distracting for the team. Discussions of a possible merger or sale of the bank could, at a minimum, disrupt performance and could also lead to critical team members entertaining offers from the competition. There was much at stake in having this meeting. The board could question my passion and desire for running the bank by broaching the topic, or they could decide this was an appropriate action to explore. There were no guarantees where any of this discussion would go, so it was important from my perspective to limit attendance to those only with a need to know. Our management team, who always attended our board meetings, was not there. Just our board and the investment bankers we had chosen to potentially take us on this journey. The meeting minutes and the meeting minutes from subsequent meetings related to this project were kept by me and held in strict confidence. I played the role of corporate secretary for these meetings. The minutes would later need to become a part of the corporate record.

The investment bankers made a presentation to the board covering the various strategic options the bank had: staying the same, buying somebody, merging with an equal, or a sale. An overview of the current bank M&A environment was provided, and key trends were discussed along with deal drivers. The pluses and minuses were discussed for each of the strategic options. There was a good give and take between the board and the investment bankers on the various aspects of each of the options. The investment bankers discussed acquisition targets and merger candidate filtering along with best practices as well.

An in-depth valuation range was discussed. A broad potential buyer list was presented based on the investment banker's market intelligence as a starting point for discussions on potential buyers. The process was discussed in detail as well as potential timing for beginning and the various steps along the way all the way through to closing.

As the questions were answered, the investment bankers were thanked and excused to allow for a private discussion by the board to review the options presented to us. After an extensive and robust discussion, the board opted to make a request of the investment bankers for an engagement letter to function as the sole and exclusive financial advisor to the holding company to explore a potential sale.

The next step was to engage legal counsel for the potential sale. They would also review the investment banker's engagement letter. Following review of the engagement letter by legal counsel, and added negotiation with the investment bankers, the final form of the engagement letter was then distributed to the board for final review and approval. All-in the process described above took about five business days, following the meeting with the board.

Without getting into the specifics of our engagement, generally, an engagement of this type will be exclusive. The investment bankers also would like the names of any potential purchaser that had been in contact at any point in the past so that there wouldn't be any confusion going forward about exclusivity. They don't want a party to later claim they had already been in contact and had been in discussions prior to investment bankers' engagement and not subject to their fee.

Fees are generally based upon success and are typically tied to the total purchase price in the form of a percentage, generally in the range of as little as 1.5% to as much as 4% (again, this is very general, based upon the circumstances of the proposed transaction, and subject to negotiation), plus expenses (travel, meals, lodging, document production, etc.) limited to a negotiated amount.

At this point, the only people who are knowledgeable of the potential sale is the board.

Confidentiality is critical throughout the process to protect the shareholders, employees, and customers of the bank.

Any whisper of a potential sale will potentially decrease the value of the shares and will have competitors calling our employees and trying to poach our customers.

The board has an implicit confidentiality agreement. We also had outside counsel put together a formal Insider Agreement to be signed by each board member, reminding and heightening awareness to the sensitivity of the circumstances. This is a practice I believe everyone should do. The investment bankers told the board that whenever word had gotten out in past engagements, or engagements they were familiar with, the leak was generally traced back to a board member having a casual conversation with a friend or a board member's spouse who later shared the information with others. We'll talk about the Insider Agreement in the next chapter and having the board sign was valuable there relative to the internal "deal team."

I am not a lawyer, so it is strongly recommended that you seek legal counsel on your Insider Agreement.

We now had approval from our board who is knowledgeable about our value range, strategic options and the current market conditions in bank M&A, we have hired our legal counsel and investment bankers (accounting firm, as previously mentioned, was already engaged) and we are about to set out assembling an initial interest packet for distribution, identifying potentially interested parties, having one-on-one meetings, supplying additional information, and answering questions to see what the market thinks.

NOTE: If you are at this stage, you are **roughly one-year away from closing**, assuming the most efficient path to closing. You may be done sooner, but there is a greater likelihood it will be longer rather than shorter.

Let's now focus on the deal team and gathering our initial round of data for due diligence.

CHAPTER 14

DEAL TEAM AND DATA ROOM

W e had a small but highly effective board of five people. This is provided for perspective. There is no right or wrong answer for the size of your board. Ours happened to be the minimum size allowed by state statutes as we were a state-chartered bank. We felt that size was more efficient for us. Three outside board members and two inside board members, myself (chairman and CEO) and our president. Because we were only 16 years old, we both wore many hats throughout our time there. So, there was more day-to-day knowledge between the two of us inside board members in all aspects of the bank than a more long-standing bank would typically have with a more traditional "silo" structure. The side benefit of that was that we would keep our "deal team" limited in size. As more of the management team was hired and developed, the number of hats each of the two of us were wearing decreased. Despite handing over those duties, we still maintained a very good understanding of what was happening throughout the bank.

Because of the highly sensitive nature of the project, the deal team consists of only those who need to be included in the process and is only added to on an as-needed basis. At that point, only our board had knowledge of the project. As mentioned in the last chapter, we have been informally interviewing our potential investment banking partners for several years up to this point.

We were formed as a C-corporation so that we could have IRA investors. IRA investors need to provide their custodians with annual stock valuations. Because of this, we had a stock valuation performed each year by an independent third party and we provided a copy of that valuation to all shareholders. The valuation provided was for a minority interest, a lesser percentage of the majority share value.

We changed providers every few years to ensure we had objective reviews and to allow for us to again, "try-out" firms we were informally "interviewing" as potential investment banking partners. As fortune would have it, the firm we had chosen to be our advisor on this project was selected to provide our annual valuation six months prior to the board's decision to pursue this project.

That engagement allowed us to request much more information from our people than we would typically provide for our valuations as we were bringing a new valuation provider up to speed. So that, along with the fact that we had finished our exam cycle just prior to our board meeting to discuss the project, allowed for the investment bankers to have quite a bit of current information to form the valuation range that was provided to the board.

My point in bringing this up is that the makeup of your "deal team" will depend upon your individual circumstances. You may need to include your chief credit officer earlier in the process. You may need to include your lead IT person earlier in the process. Or you may need to include your human resources lead in the process. Your situation will be unique to you and your depths of understanding of the details of your bank.

At this point, our president could answer most, if not all, questions about our individual commercial customer relationships as well as our overall loan portfolio credit quality down to each specific borrower. So, we didn't need to bring our chief commercial officer or our chief credit officer into the mix, or "under the tent" as it is often referred to.

We would need to go even further on the financial side than the information that was provided for the valuation, and because of that, it was now time to bring our chief financial officer under the tent.

You never really know how a meeting about bringing somebody under the tent will go until you have it. But we had done some things prior to this that hopefully would mitigate the risk associated with that conversation. Primarily, it was a general understanding amongst the management team that this was a business. We emphasized that we were building shareholder value. We emphasized the differences in stakeholder value and shareholder value. We also emphasized that capital follows value and that we were developing a competent and skilled team. The team was managing a project that happened to be a bank. We wanted team members to be aware of the value they were building for themselves that nobody could ever take from them. Your fears in bringing any employees under the tent are that the word will get out and the value of the bank will go down. Employees may seek employment elsewhere or customers may come under even greater competitive pressure to leave. Additionally, your fear is that an employee will lose focus and not be as engaged as they had been up to that point.

This is another reason why the Change-In-Control agreements with your key people are so valuable to the bank and its shareholders. Those same key people have a great deal to benefit from a change-in-control that can even serve to heighten engagement and confidentiality of the process. The Stay-Put feature also ensures they have a very cooperative stance with the buyers in the long run rather than taking on an "us versus them" stance.

Although the Change-In-Control agreements have confidentiality clauses in them, having an Insider Agreement signed as an added emphasis is also a great reminder. Being able to say that each board member has signed an Insider Agreement goes a long way to affirm buy-in.

I am not a lawyer, so it is strongly recommended that you seek legal counsel on your Insider Agreement.

So, if you're keeping count, at this point we have three insiders (chairman and CEO, president, and chief financial officer) as the deal team. We will now need to begin the process of fulfilling the data request from the investment bankers, beyond the initial request associated with the valuation project mentioned earlier.

The investment bankers gather the information electronically, review the information, and ask any questions they may have as a result, and begin populating the virtual data room that will become the source of information for potentially interested parties at various points along the way. That same data room will ultimately serve as the data room for the entire process through closing. The investment bankers manage the credentials throughout the process and the collection of the agreements to view the information, as we will cover in Chapter 19 – Non-Disclosure Agreements (NDAs).

This service is another major reason why using an investment banker is so valuable to the project. You have a bank to run, and that means your people's time is very valuable. Having a team behind you that can handle this is critical on many fronts.

We will expand the deal team a bit further as you will learn in Chapter 22 – Further Data and Deal Team Expansion, but for now the team is still very limited.

With the data in the process of being gathered for review by *potentially interested parties* we begin focusing on who those parties may be based upon *how we want to approach the market* and we'll discuss that in the next chapter.

CHAPTER 15

POTENTIALLY INTERESTED PARTIES

G enerally, there are three ways to approach taking the bank to market.

The **first approach** is a very discreet approach. I call it the "**one buyer**" approach. You have a buyer lined up and you have very confidential negotiations with just one party. This may be somebody you have become close to through the years, you think a lot alike, perhaps have shared participations back and forth and have a high degree of comfort with. This is the most discreet, but probably won't deliver the best value in the long run and could also open you up to criticism by the shareholders regarding maximizing the value of their investment. Shareholders may be drawn to the idea that having negotiated only with one party; they aren't so sure value was maximized. Or perhaps there was something in it for management that comes at the expense of the shareholders. Something like a cherry role with significant compensation and benefits.

A **second approach**, on the other end of the spectrum, is to hold an auction. I call it the "**one-bid**" approach. Invite many potential buyers to the process and have a set date on which offers are accepted. The bank goes to the highest bidder. Certainly not discreet and you are exposed to a whole host of risks with employees and customers.

This also may not deliver the highest price. This could open another avenue of criticism by the shareholders as the value may be damaged by this very public process.

The **third approach** is to invite more to the party than one buyer, but not broadcast the event as an auction or have a hard and fast winner-takes-all, one-time bid, format. I call this the "**strategic**" approach. This approach is more discreet than an auction, with one-on-one conversations with several potential buyers, and control of the competitive process along the way. Our investment banker referred to it as the "Goldilocks" approach, not too little, not too many, the "just right" approach.

Our board decided on the third approach, the strategic approach, so that is the approach my comments will focus on. This strategic approach will be our focus and will take us through to Chapter 27 – Letter of Intent (LOI) and Board Approval.

To begin this process, we were just figuring out who might be interested in having a conversation. There is a tendency to think too far ahead or to think too competitively at this point in the process. You may get in your own way by thinking your bank wouldn't be the right fit for this *other* bank, or by thinking *There's no way we'd want to be a part of that bank*. Maybe because you've been such tough competitors throughout the years, and you can't bear the thought of it.

Those fears might end up being true in the future, but now's not the time to make that call. Now's the time to be as open in your thought process as you can about who may have an interest in talking. Also, if you have hired a bank sell-side M&A investment banker, they are having conversations daily with people and may have some insight into somebody you would have discounted or somebody who is significantly larger but is trying to enter your market and would perhaps be interested.

Your primary goal, as we have covered in Chapter 11 – Shareholders, is your fiduciary responsibility to your shareholders: maximizing shareholder value.

About credit unions: Many banks spend their entire existence fighting against credit unions. You are exercising your fiduciary responsibilities in fighting them as competition. It does impact shareholder value maximization. But you have a fiduciary responsibility to your shareholders in the sales process as well that trumps your personal feelings. This is a very interesting dilemma bank CEOs face and requires compartmentalization. There may be other things down the road that throw them out of the mix as a buyer, but until that point, don't discount them as potentially interested in acquiring your bank.

Unless there is a reason you can stand behind that protects you from breaching your fiduciary responsibilities of duty, loyalty, and care in maximizing shareholder value from not holding a meeting with an interested party, keep an open mind. Your goal with this project is to have as many conversations as you can.

It's like any sales process. You must fill the top of the funnel with many prospects to have a few make it out of the funnel.

At this point, nobody has been contacted yet. No information will go out specifically about your bank until confidentiality agreements, or non-disclosure agreements as we'll refer to them, NDAs for short, have been collected (we will cover these in Chapter 19 – Non-Disclosure Agreements).

So, once we come up with the list, how do we contact them? We'll cover that in the next chapter.

CHAPTER 16

COUNTERPARTY OUTREACH

This chapter assumes you have hired an investment banker to help you with the process. This counterparty outreach—calling potentially interested parties to see if they are "interested" parties—is done on your behalf by the investment bankers.

During this process, the investment bankers contact each of the identified potentially interested parties and have a very high-level conversation about their appetite for an acquisition. At this point, names are not used to protect your bank from widespread industry awareness that you are for sale. A brief description, often referred to as a "teaser," is provided about the opportunity to decide if they would like to move to the next step. To describe this process over the next few chapters, I am going to take you through the classic sales model of Attention, Interest, Desire, and Action (AIDA). The model helps demonstrate where you are in the sales process.

- **Attention**: Before something can happen, you need to get the potential buyer's attention. Who are you? Why should they listen?

- **Interest**: Just because you have their attention doesn't mean they are interested. This is the stage where you are attempting to capture their interest. What does this have to do with us?

- **Desire**: This is the stage where you are trying to take them from "I <u>like</u> this" to "I <u>want</u> this." How will this help make our lives easier, or better?

- **Action**: This is the goal where you are moving them to the stage where they are taking action. They are moving from "I <u>want</u> this" to "I <u>need</u> this."

The investment bankers have gotten them through the <u>attention stage</u> from their historical work with the potential buyer along with the authority they have built over years in dealing with the industry. Without an investment banker this stage alone could be difficult for a banker to act on their own behalf. Getting potential buyers' attention on your own, just to get the process started, could prove to be very difficult. Let alone trying to get the attention of several potential buyers.

The investment bankers are trying to move them to the <u>interest stage</u>.

As you can imagine, the stages of getting attention and interest are labor intensive. The process is a lot of phone calls, emails, texts, and follow-up calls, follow-up emails, and follow-up texts. There is a great deal of information gleaned by the investment bankers about the deal that is being discussed, but also in general about the acquirer's current state of mind.

The message goes something like this (completely fabricated by me for illustration purposes only):

"We have an opportunity for a possible acquisition by your bank in a major Midwest metropolitan market. The size of the bank is approximately $250 million. Focus is on C&I, working capital lines of credit, term loans and owner-occupied real estate. Treasury management is also an area of focus. The management team is a strength, can aid in management succession, have CICs and Stay-Puts in place. The board is exploring their strategic options, a sale being one of them as they understand the power of scale. Strong bank, good earner, solid team in a high-growth market that fits nicely with your footprint. We thought of you. Are you interested?"

That conversation builds goodwill with the buyer on behalf of the sell-side investment bankers. The buyer, if they are a serious acquirer, will want to think twice before saying no to ensure they continue to hear about opportunities from the sell-side banker. Both of those things help you. The longer they stay in the process, the more opportunity you have. The more potentially interested parties you have in the process, the better the opportunity you have. You want as many interested parties as possible at this point in the process. Don't worry about whether it is a strategic fit—figuring that out comes later. There also may be somebody who you saw as the best fit in the world that passed—you may be thinking, *But if they only knew it was us!* That may happen, but you can't worry about it. You must keep moving. If you really want them to know, I encourage you to talk with the investment bankers about a strategy for attempting to contact them a little further down the road. You may also find out the reason they provided has nothing to do with you. It has to do with them. Keep moving forward.

For perspective, we had 48 on our potentially interested party list for the investment bankers to call. Your number could be more or could be less. The point here isn't to focus on the actual number. Again, it is to provide perspective. We had 15 interested parties that opted to move to the next step. So, about 30%, which is a typical percentage.

Again, this is why you want to fill the top of the funnel up when building the list. This process took about 30 days and should be about what you should expect.

Reasons given not moving on were:

- Too small.

- Buyer not currently acquisitive.

- Timing.

- Insufficient ability to manage the opportunity right now.

- Metropolitan market not a fit.

- The geography wasn't a fit—too far away.

- The market served wasn't a match.

- Culture wasn't a fit. Rural bank not wanting to go into a metro market.

- Transaction costs would be too much.

- The branch network wasn't large enough.

- Acquisition would result in concentrations of borrowers, like lending to a particular industry, or increasing leasing or residential construction beyond comfort, or by geography as examples.

- A Community Development Financial Institution (CDFI) acquirer and acquisition would change the CDFI calculation area, possibly jeopardizing their CDFI designation. A CDFI is a private financial institution whose primary mission is to help communities that are traditionally left out of banking options.

As you can see, there was nothing personal listed. There were no right or wrong answers either, just rationale as to why the opportunity wasn't right at the time.

Let's keep going with those who <u>are</u> interested.

Reasons why potential buyers are interested:

- The acquisition would be just the right size for us.

- We are seeking another bank to buy right now.

- The timing is good from a project standpoint for our team.

- The market is a good fit.

- The geography is a good fit for our footprint.

- The market served is a good match for us (could be demographics, or a product match).

- Their culture is a good fit with ours.

- They have a branch network we like.

What happens next?

The next step is to get together for one-on-one meetings to begin the identification process and move them from the "<u>interest</u>" stage to the "<u>desire</u>" stage on the path to <u>acting</u> on that desire.

We'll cover that in the next chapter.

CHAPTER 17

ONE-ON-ONE MEETINGS

N ow that conversations have taken place with the list of potentially interested parties, it's time to move to the next step of sharing more about the opportunity. It's time for one-on-one meetings. That means you now need to help them move to the "desire" stage: building their desire to go further through the process.

The one-on-one meetings could be formal or informal. They could happen at a conference over lunch, or dinner, or drinks. They could even take place during or between conference sessions. My preference was to keep them batched, if possible. What I mean by batched is much the same fashion I would make sales calls. Two or three a day was my preference for sales calls. It allowed for more efficient and productive meetings. Personally, I was indifferent as to whether the meetings were formal or informal as I am comfortable with both settings. You may have a preference. The meeting was the important part for me, regardless of the setting. There was a tempo that developed, and you can cover a fair amount of ground in a relatively short number of days. Your investment banker will want to sit in on the meetings too, so having them batched together accommodates travel schedules better as well. The reason they want to sit in on them is not to guide your conversation, but rather to continue learning your history and thought process so they can answer questions from buyers more efficiently further along in the process.

Your preference could be entirely different, and that's up to you and your investment banker.

There are tips I would pass along to help your meetings go well:

- The meeting generally lasts about an hour or as much as two hours. The time generally goes by very quickly and follows a format much like this:

  o Introductions & Pleasantries

    ▪ Investment bankers take the lead if the parties aren't familiar with one another. If you and the potential buyer are familiar with one another, the pleasantries likely begin immediately and at some comfortable point in the conversation. The investment banker will move on to the meeting agenda.

  o Meeting Agenda

    ▪ Investment bankers take the lead.

      - The investment banker will ask if there is any backend time pressure to be concerned about. Knowing about this in advance of the meeting is helpful in determining how quickly to hit on important message points. Ideally, there is no time pressure, but occasionally there is. This is also helpful to establish up front because if the potential buyer says they have time pressure, then later says "No, keep going, I will adjust my schedule" you have a clear indication that interest is being established. If they say they have no backend time pressure, then into the meeting they suddenly remember they have an upcoming meeting they had forgotten, that is another cue, only this time it's a cue that they are not interested.

- Discuss how the meeting came about (e.g., the board has engaged us to review strategic options and report back to them what we find. At this point, they are not certain what path this may take, but selling could be a choice. We know you (the buyer), have a great deal of respect for what you have built, and thought there might be a benefit to introducing the two parties to see where it might go.)

■ From there, the banker may ask you to give a little background on:

- The bank and holding company (if applicable):

    o Brief history

        ■ How the bank got started

        ■ Total asset size

        ■ Geographic footprint

        ■ Area(s) of focus (e.g., consumer, commercial, commercial real estate, agriculture, or residential construction and mortgage lending)

        ■ Culture

        ■ Strengths

        ■ Talent

- Shareholder base (in general, e.g., family-owned, widely held, closely held, possibly mention concentrations without going into specific detail)

  - More recent history or trends

- Your background:

  o Keep in mind the bank is the star of the show.

  o It's okay to highlight your career, but my advice is to make sure it doesn't sound like you're interviewing for a job (i.e., a *balance* of quiet confidence and being friendly).

  o Sprinkle in your authority throughout the meeting. You don't want this to appear as if the bank's value is dependent on you. That may make you feel good but will bring the value of the bank down. If you are the whole key to the bank's value, please go back and reread Chapter 9 – Talent.

  o Highlight the talent around you helping you to be successful, give them credit. Balance is the key, don't go overboard or oversell here either. That can appear disingenuous.

    - This likely will raise the question of whether your team will be willing to stay if the bank is bought. Be prepared for that question – CICs could be mentioned here if they are in place. Also, a larger organization may be great for your people to continue to extend their skills and careers.

- Answer questions as they come up throughout this part of the conversation.

  o An interactive conversation or just quiet, intense listening on behalf of the other party could each be great signs they are interested.

  o Conversely, watch for a lot of body movement and shifting in their chair. It could be a sign you're droning on about a topic and need to shift to another topic. Your investment banker may be watching for this too, to help guide a transition to another topic.

■ The investment banker will likely then move on to the next part of the agenda, asking the acquirer if they would take some time to describe their background, history, culture, and any additional thoughts they would like to highlight.

- Ask questions during this part of the conversation that fit with the conversation. In other words, stay on topic or go off topic but stay at the level of the conversation. If it's a 40,000-foot overview, stay at that level or maybe go down a level or two (30,000 feet or 20,000 feet) but avoid going too detailed (down a rabbit hole or asking them to reveal strategies they wouldn't to a competitor). Something like, "What's your strategy for building out your treasury management function?" Or "Who is your number one rainmaker on the commercial side of things?" In general, stay away from things you would feel uncomfortable saying to the competition.

- Stay engaged, again with a *balance* of quiet confidence and being friendly.

- Following those discussions, the investment banker may ask both sides if there are any other questions each has.

- Following that, the investment banker may inquire a bit further about the buyer's interest level if they pick up on something in the meeting. Or may ask about deal criteria the buyer has previously used to gauge the buyer's interest. An answer where the buyer is "leaning in" talking with energy about possible deal structure could be interpreted by a savvy investment banker as a sign of interest in your deal.

- This isn't an exhaustive review of all that you could cover in these meetings, but it's close.

- Do your homework on their operation prior to the meeting. None of this information may come up in this first meeting but do your homework so you can begin piecing together your picture of the acquirer. Even if you have known the acquirer for some time, you are most likely approaching this from a completely different angle at this point and will want to get as much of a picture in your mind as possible.

o A good investment banker will provide you with a packet of information on the prospective buyer well in advance of your meeting so you can be informed on the public data available on the institution.

o Search the Internet for articles on the person you're meeting with to gather as much insight as you can from that as well.

o Research social media accounts on the person you're meeting with as well. Both personal accounts and business accounts.

o Look for articles on any acquisition they have done recently, to see what the quotes from the leaders are focused on.

o Search the Internet for more information on the owners, or ownership.

o Search LinkedIn for employees you may be familiar with.

o If you have a subscription to S&P Global, or your investment bankers do, look up their ownership and ownership percentages so you can possibly determine who the decision makers are. You will find this information, if the potential buyer has a holding company, by requesting a copy of their FR Y-6 report (Annual Report of Holding Companies) filed with the potential buyer's supervisory Federal Reserve Bank. Going this route is a fairly laborious process, and you have to wait for the information to be mailed to you. Once you have a copy of the FR Y-6, research the individuals in the report for any information that may provide insight as to the buyer's plans. That insight could show you that the bank is a small part of the majority shareholder's holdings, possibly indicating the bank is more likely to be a long-term hold. It could indicate the opposite as well, that the investment in the bank represents the bulk of the majority shareholder's wealth. If so, it may lead to asking questions down the road related to how the majority shareholder plans to liquidate their holdings (this is a question for consideration after offers come in and you are deciding between options, and in particular if it is an all-stock or a partial stock transaction). There are no certain answers here, but there are clues that can lead to asking questions that could reveal more clues. Those clues can aid in finding the motivation for their interest and your ability to position for more value.

o   If they are publicly traded, look at their most recent filings, 10-K and/or 10-Q for any added insight you may be able to gather.

• Your meeting will likely be of a higher-level, get-to-know-your-style kind of meeting. That means it's not the place for them to delve too deeply into any non-public information with you yet. Your investment banker may step in if the meeting is headed that way, but it has been my experience that the buyers know NDAs have not been signed yet and that level of conversation isn't appropriate yet either. If the conversation does go in that direction and your investment banker is not there or doesn't speak up, just politely let the person know you'll be happy to provide that information when NDAs have been signed and it's appropriate. Types of questions about large customers or specifics about strategies and/or pricing or details on key personnel are the kinds of questions I am referring to.

- Conversely, don't expect to hear the strategies and inner workings of the potential acquirer either. Again, this is a "get-to-know-you" meeting. You can push for some answers to see how accommodating they may be with information but do so politely and back off at any sign of discomfort with your questions. You don't want to turn them off.

- Keep in mind that you are not being judgmental about them in any way. The whole purpose of this meeting is to get another meeting. There is time later for making decisions between potential acquirers later. Now is not that time. It is okay to have judgments, share them with your investment bankers, note them for later consideration, but don't dismiss any interested party at this point. It's too early for that, there will be an opportunity to bring that back into the discussion later on.

- If you don't come from a sales background, you need to practice your story. Practice it until you can say it in your sleep so you can pay attention to cues you may be getting from the acquirer. Watch for those cues on when to add more or when to move on. You need to know how to break when they are engaged and want to ask a question, so you don't lose that engagement. During my sales days, I was taught that when the customer is nodding their head yes when you're talking, hand them the pen and shut up. His advice was, you have answered the questions they were looking for, so it's time to move on. The last thing you want to do is to drone on and turn a yes into a no.

Practice it with your investment bankers if you need to. They have been involved in hundreds of these conversations. They know how to read them. Take their advice between meetings and don't take offense if they tell you to change something. There is a lot riding on these meetings.

If you are the chairman or CEO and your president is more of a salesperson than you are, you may wish to have them in the meeting providing that piece of information with you stepping in to answer questions periodically. The one-on-one meeting is more art than science. If it's not your strong suit, figure out how you will make accommodation for that.

A copywriter I have high regard for says, "The job of the first sentence is to get you to read the second sentence. The job of the second sentence is to get you to read the third, and so on." When he is asked how long the copy needs to be, he says you need to say enough to get them to buy and not one word more. This is another reference to keep in the back of your mind while going through this process. Avoid oversharing, but you do have to provide enough to keep things moving in the right direction.

Your sole focus at this point is to arrange for another meeting.

- Remember they are interested in meeting you, or if you've met prior, learning more about you and your bank, that's why they're there.

- They are thinking "Do & Become" so you need to know the answers to:

  o Why do you want to sell?

  o Will your employees stay?

  o Will your customers stay?

  o Why would joining us work?

- They will politely listen to you discuss your culture; they will want to hear about it once to see if it meshes with theirs. Beyond that they have their own culture. They are not looking for somebody to come in and change it. That's something you need to be respectful of. I know your job is likely the keeper of the culture and you will naturally want to go there. Go there once. Then listen when they talk about their culture, nod, and agree. Now is not the time for anything other than that.

- Having said all of that, the most important thing is to be yourself and enjoy the meeting.

  o If you're not ready to be yourself and enjoy the meeting, figure out how you're going to get there and get working on it!

And remember… You've got this.

CHAPTER 18

BOARD REVIEW AND REQUESTS FOR OFFERS

Y ou've concluded all your one-on-one meetings, and it is time to survey the landscape with the board.

We're about to see if the interested parties have moved to the "desire" stage in this process.

Your investment bankers will likely lead this meeting with your board. This is great because it offers the board an opportunity to hear from observers of the meetings rather than from you. Your comments may be perceived as having a bias towards a party or parties where *your* post-deal interests may be better served.

Remember the fiduciary duty of the board is to maximize shareholder value, as it is the shareholders' interests that are to be served. This is also another great benefit of working with investment bankers because they can provide that objective perspective, erasing any doubts board members and/or shareholders may have. It provides protection for you.

Because so much time has passed since the board has heard about the activity in the deal, the investment bankers will take a few minutes to review the transaction timeline with them for perspective.

Since engaging the investment bankers, you have:

- Done an internal due diligence with them so they can prepare themselves for representation of the bank.

- You have collaborated on a universe of potentially interested parties for contacting.

- The outreach process took place to determine if the parties are interested in a one-on-one meeting.

- You have had one-on-one meetings with each interested party.

- Those who have expressed a desire to continue to talk have been thanked for their interest and it is now time to move to the next level.

- It is time to enlighten them further with a deeper look and to assess their true desires by asking them to make an offer in writing.

As a reminder, the chapters in this book are the entire process in chronological order. You can look at the table of contents as the process map.

The board will also be apprised of the process going forward to allow them to create a mental timeline of events to prompt or to answer questions. For now, the interest level has been determined, there may be a straggler or two that pop up down the road, but for the most part you have identified those who have an interest.

The next step is to determine what that level of interest is and how committed they are to the process. Is it a *"confirmation* yes"? Or a *"commitment* yes"? Have they *entered* the *"desire"* stage?

A "confirmation yes" is generally innocent, a reflex, just a simple affirmation with *no promise of action.*

A "commitment yes" is the real deal; it's a true agreement that *leads to action.*

In the process of raising capital for the bank, I encountered this frequently. There are direct communicators and there are indirect communicators. There is no "right" or "wrong" communication style, but you do need to know if you are speaking with a direct communicator or an indirect communicator. If you go through as many meetings trying to raise money to start a bank, as I have, your skill level of determining which type you're talking with goes up significantly.

The next step is to try to determine just that. Who are the *truly* interested parties? Which parties have entered the "desire" stage? The "I need this" stage.

So, the next step is for the investment bankers to ask each of the parties to sign a confidentiality agreement, often referred to as a non-disclosure agreement or NDA. For our purposes, we will be referring to them as an NDA but know the two are interchangeable.

An NDA is a document that is exchanged between a prospective buyer and seller after the prospective buyer shows an interest in the bank. The objective of the NDA is to make sure the party receiving the confidential information doesn't use that information for its own benefit.

The interested parties are asked to demonstrate their level of commitment to the process by signing the NDA, receiving information they will need to provide a *non-binding* offer. A quick deadline for receiving offers is set as well, usually just a week or two following, so truly interested parties will go through the process and those who were a confirmation yes are provided the opportunity to excuse themselves. Most of those who opt not to proceed still do sign the NDA and are able to see the data provided.

Once an NDA is signed, the acquirer will be provided with a Confidential Information Memorandum or "CIM" (often referred to as and pronounced "sim"). Provided in the CIM is a roadmap of next steps in the process, some higher-level supporting information. Also, in the CIM is a table of contents for the deeper dive information they have access to in the virtual data room.

What we are looking for at this point in the process is to determine who is serious and who is not.

In this process, a great deal of information is shared. Things such as strategic plans, corporate organizational structure, financial information, characteristics of the loan portfolio, other real estate owned (OREO), the investment portfolio, deposit composition, other liabilities, management, and personnel including compensation, materials contracts, and insurance coverage as well as the branches and facilities information.

It is the information you would want to see to put together an offer so that the offer is credible and both parties know it is in the ballpark where the best and final offer would be. This is a dance, and with experienced advisors on both sides, a very well-choreographed dance at that. It isn't in anybody's best interest for this process not to be efficient.

If represented by an investment banker, there will be strict instructions not to contact anybody at the bank directly.

That includes you, any directors, or any employees. All questions should go through the investment bankers, and they will retrieve the answers and respond. If you are not using an investment banker, you will be fielding all these calls. Think of it as being the single point of contact for multiple regulatory exams taking place at the same time. The investment bankers field the questions, answer as many of them as they can, pass along the questions that the subject matter experts on your deal team can answer. The subject matter experts get the answers back to the investment bankers to communicate back to the buyer's team. Only those questions that remain following the process are the questions that need your attention. You provide those answers again, to your own investment bankers to communicate back to the other side(s).

Because offers are often assembled to make it harder to compare one another side-by-side, instructions are provided on the format of the offer. This is done by the buyers, as you would expect, to keep offers from being a side-by-side comparison reduced solely in terms of price. My guess is you have tried to fashion your offers to prospects and customers like this in the past as well. The bidders are trying to appeal to the issues they feel they can make a difference, such as roles for management or calculations that may look appealing, but perhaps the scales would tip in the buyer's favor upon closer review, or closer to closing. Investment bankers, particularly sell-side bank M&A advisors, can sort through these things and point out anything that is outside of what they normally see. There is an opportunity for buyers to color outside the lines in additional documentation following what is required in the format, but the investment bankers provide tremendous value here too in comparing apples-to-apples once the offers are submitted so that the board can be more efficient in their decision-making.

The next chapter will provide a little more insight into what's in an NDA.

CHAPTER 19

NON-DISCLOSURE AGREEMENTS

O kay, you've heard about the confidentiality agreement or non-disclosure agreement (NDA) a few times now. Here is where they fit into the timeline and here is what they do (reminder, I'm not a lawyer and suggest you speak with your lawyer about any questions you may have). I am going to refer to the agreement from this point on as the NDA.

The objective of the NDA is to make sure the party receiving the confidential information doesn't use the information for their own benefit. Customer names, employee names, compensation information and other sensitive data like this are what is at risk. A well-written NDA typically includes the covenant that confidential information may only be "used solely for the purpose of evaluation of the potential transaction" or words to that effect.

NDAs usually exclude certain information which doesn't amount to a breach of the confidential clause. Some exceptions are:

- Information about this already in the public domain.

- Information that the disclosing party disclosed prior to signing the agreement.

- Information that was received by a third party where the third-party was not obliged to keep the information confidential.

- Information that was in the lawful possession of the receiving party before the date of the signing.

The disclosing party should always want to include a provision that all information, including physical and electronic data, should be destroyed if the parties terminate negotiations. However, the receiving party generally negotiates this clause with the disclosing party and reaches the conclusion that the destruction of such records does not apply to their internal recordkeeping, and any electronic backup storage or professional recordkeeping.

An NDA is only as strong as the checkbook prepared to defend it. That is my belief and the same goes for most legal agreements. The biggest checkbook usually wins as it can provide the most vigorous argument or delay the process until you run out of cash.

Now, having said that upfront, I will say the NDA here has a little bit more to it than meets the eye. And that is reputation risk on the party that breaches the NDA. An acquirer, especially a serial acquirer or an acquirer with aspirations of many acquisitions to perhaps build out or complete a geographic footprint as an example, certainly does not want their reputation tainted with a breach. They will see a slowdown of new opportunity deal flow that slows to a trickle if not being completely shut off.

That gives me some comfort. I know it's not perfect, but it does carry weight in my book.

Within the NDA, are some very good provisions that you want to make certain yours carries as well. It's up to you and your lawyers to get this done.

Typical NDAs prevent the signers, for a period of (generally) two years, from:

- Disclosing anything about the contemplated transaction.

- Disclosing they are having conversations with you about the transaction.

- Disclosing they are evaluating anything regarding the transaction.

- Soliciting an employee.

- Hiring an employee.

- They won't directly or indirectly contact any customers, clients, or partners, of whom they became aware of through the evaluation materials.

These are just a few of the terms being agreed to, generally, and this is not complete—just some highlights for reference.

This chapter is very brief and could have easily been a part of the preceding chapter. I wanted it to remain a separate chapter for emphasis. An agreement like an NDA could just get lumped in with all the typical boilerplate legal agreements. I think this serves as an example where the implications of this particular agreement go beyond what the agreement actually says. There is heavy reputation risk tied to this agreement that goes beyond this transaction, or the size of the potential buyer's resources.

For that reason, I thought it deserved its own chapter.

Keep in mind I am not a lawyer, so it is strongly recommended you seek legal counsel on your NDAs.

CHAPTER 20

MANAGING THE BANK

Are you feeling unfaithful? Don't worry. That's normal. To me it was very uncomfortable because my management style is pretty much an open book. As an open book leader, I felt as though I was not being truthful with the team. My duties were to the shareholders and what I was doing was in line with those duties. There was nothing untoward about it, but I preferred being able to share what we were doing with the team. It can provide you some solace to know that the team that helped build value for the bank would participate in that value realization through their CICs and Stay-Put agreements if you have those in place.

From a strategic perspective, the meetings with the investment bankers didn't feel that way because that was my job. Looking out over the next three to five years to chart our course was standard work. Then it became a little more real. The one-on-one meetings with interested parties ramped up that feeling.

Now, you are really exposing information and you undoubtedly will feel uncomfortable. There is a great deal at stake, even more so if you have significant ownership in the bank and your future depends on it for your family. But you also care about all the other families affected by what is happening here as well, and that all starts to weigh very heavily. And it only gets heavier from here, so buckle up!

You must set all of that aside and manage the bank.

You must manage the bank as if none of this is happening.

You must.

The sale may not happen.

The passage of time only adds risk into the equation every day.

What if the market collapses and attention is turned elsewhere?

We just came through a pandemic—what if something like that were to happen again?

What if the offers are way below the value range that was expected?

This process would be all pushed aside and just be a footnote in the history of the bank. The bank needs to continue to deliver for the shareholders, the customers, your employees, and the community.

Naturally, you begin to think, we won't need to worry about this issue or that issue because somebody else will be making that call. But you must resist those thoughts at all costs and continue with the same decision-making you would have if the process weren't taking place. It helped me to visualize the deal going away and having to defend any decision being made. The audience for that message wouldn't have knowledge of the deal, and if you referenced that there was a deal in play, and that you conditioned your decision on it going through and it didn't, you would look foolish. You would not be proud of that answer and couldn't defend it. Earlier in my career, I was a part of an organization who made short-term decisions because it was their desire to position themselves for sale. They were gaming the short-term because they felt they would not have to be responsible for their decisions in the long-term. It wasn't something that was overtly stated, but it didn't take a genius to see what was happening. Well, that seller never sold, and that management is no longer with them. I don't like to use absolutes, but never assume something will happen in business.

The same holds true for shareholders selling their shares. You cannot mention what is happening. It may not happen. Those transactions need to be allowed to continue as if this process were not taking place.

Building maintenance and repairs, re-topping and striping the parking lot, watering the lawn, replacing worn furniture and equipment, computer system upgrades and security, employee raises—they all need to happen as if there will be no sale. One reason for this is that the sale may never happen, and a second reason is even if it does happen, it is the right thing to do. If you were buying a bank and noticed they were letting the grass turn brown, the parking lot was going into disrepair and things were generally beginning to get tired, what would your reaction be? It would likely be either, "I'm not interested anymore," or "We must put in more money than we thought after we buy it, so we need to lower our offer."

Besides, what was just mentioned is not going to have an immediate impact on your current year's earnings, as it will be put on a depreciation or amortization schedule and won't affect your offer/purchase price.

You're also concerned about the risk of the process while you're managing the bank.

What if word of this were to get out?

What if a key employee, even one protected by a CIC, decided to move on? Where would that leave us, and who could step up to replace them? Would that delay the process or change the dynamics?

What if a sizable loan, or loans, were to go the wrong direction for a currently unknown reason?

What if there was a major cybersecurity event?

You worry about these things daily, but with a potential transaction in the works, they are magnified. The only advice I can give is to stay diligent. Going back to visualizing having to defend your decision and actions if no deal ever took place.

We'll talk about managing the bank a couple more times as the process progresses from different angles.

We're about to see if any offers come in. Let's head to the next chapter to see and to see what happens then.

SECTION 3

HOW DOES THE PROCESS WORK?

CHAPTER 21

INITIAL OFFER SUBMISSION AND BOARD REVIEW

The board decided to pursue the possibility of a sale. Information has been collected, organized, and conference calls between the investment bankers have taken place to ensure that the information is a fair representation of the bank. Research has been conducted by the investment bankers to quantify the data and compare it for the potential buyers. Potential buyers have been found, contacted, and qualified. One-on-one meetings have taken place. NDAs have been collected. The CIM was developed, and the virtual data has been open for robust study. The investment banking team has fielded questions, answered many, sought answers from the deal team and responded.

You're about to get an answer to the question, "What does the market think we're worth?"

It's the moment of the big reveal.

Even though these are non-binding offers, they are still serious offers and an indication of value.

We talked about the confirmation yes and the commitment yes in Chapter 18 – Board Review and Requests for Offers.

A "confirmation yes" is generally innocent, a reflex, just a simple affirmation with no promise of action.

A "commitment yes" is the real deal, it is a true agreement that *leads* to action.

In our case, we had 11 parties who had expressed an interest in proceeding, signed NDAs and began the process of putting together a non-binding offer to meet the short deadline.

The eleven being interested in continuing the process was affirmation that the market believed we had value.

We received five written offers. Five written offers were further affirmation we had value. They were commitment yeses. Five written offers out of the 11 (45%) that indicated they wanted to move forward.

Six were confirmation yeses—55%, which is typical.

The next questions that needed to be handled were: what is that value, and is it worth continuing?

The rationale for the six opting out was very similar to the rationale we had heard when the investment bankers were calling for initial interest. An acquisition is a big step for buyers and sometimes it just takes a "live fire" drill to find reasons for them to acknowledge that now's not the time. We appreciated the fact that they thought enough of us to go this far through the process.

They had a sincere interest, and we were grateful for that.

But now it was time to focus on the offers that were received.

As mentioned in the last chapter, a specific format was supplied for the offers so that the particulars necessary for an apples-to-apples comparison could be performed by the investment bankers with the ability to add each buyer's "twist" to their offer on added pages.

As the offers came in, the investment bankers began to dissect the offers and build a spreadsheet for their study. Questions arose while deconstructing the offers that required added follow-up by the investment bankers to gain a deeper understanding of a particular element of the offer, and in a case or two, just to reaffirm the understanding of the offer.

The process of deconstructing the offer typically takes a couple of days due to the complexity and the ability to contact and hear back about questions that may arise. Once the investment bankers could communicate their findings it was time to gather the board for their presentation and to review the next steps.

Our offers were due at the close of business on a Friday. That gave the investment bankers the weekend to do their analysis. They reported their findings to me, verbally, the following Monday. We set an in-person board meeting for Wednesday for the offers to be more formally presented and any questions could be answered. In our case, the two-day lag accommodated everybody's schedule and travel for the investment bankers.

During the meeting, the investment bankers covered those key transaction terms they had specified, such as the net consideration value after all the dust had settled. It covered what that net consideration translated into on a per share basis for our shareholders and what the form of consideration was (i.e., cash, stock, or a combination of the two). If there were any contingencies, such as performance of the investment portfolio through closing, earnings, contract terminations, and such that could change the value directly between offer and closing. How the transaction expenses were accounted for in the offers and any social considerations such as severance terms, roles for the team, and board seats were also accounted for.

The analysis of the offers was then compared to the detailed valuation analysis originally performed by the investment bankers for their presentation to the board when the process started. This is an accountability piece that can be easily overlooked from my perspective. It said a great deal about the investment banking team we selected. They were not afraid to stand behind the value they presented to the board six months earlier. Right or wrong, they were making that comparison. In our case, it was right on.

For an acquisition to come together, it ultimately boils down to having a willing buyer, a willing seller, and a set of terms that all can agree on. Generally, when all three are present, it's a good time to sell. As it turned out for us, the market was telling us at that point we could be in a situation where we had a willing buyer and a willing seller.

However, we still had some work to do. Two of the offers were closer to one another and above the other three. The two offers were cash offers, similar in value, with slightly different contingencies. There were some differences in social considerations between the two offers, but the board was comfortable with either offer. The social consideration difference was that one offer had the potential for management and branding differences, where our team would be kept essentially intact to lead the charge in this market under our existing brand.

The other three offers presented had a stock or cash and stock element and the execution risk was too great for the value presented, relative to the cash offers. When this situation is presented, it is generally best to thank the three for their interest, work, and stepping up with an offer.

The next step was to move forward with the two higher, slightly separated, offers to see if one could better distance itself from the other.

There are risks involved in proceeding in this fashion.

Namely, time.

Time, as was said earlier, is generally never on your side.

CHAPTER 22

FURTHER DATA AND DEAL TEAM EXPANSION

The board decided to move forward with another offer deadline. Refining the offer further would, as one would expect, ultimately require deeper due diligence.

How much due diligence? Let's find out.

To add some perspective on the process, and to get a feel for the flow, we began with 48 potentially interested parties, which went down to 11 (23%) interested parties, and then to 5 (10%) parties who had the desire to make written offers. The numbers are going to vary for every transaction, but this should give you a general feel.

So, we had the 11 put together non-binding offers with all the data that had been initially collected. As a reminder that data were things such as, strategic plans, corporate organizational structure, financial information, characteristics of the loan portfolio, other real estate owned (OREO), the investment portfolio, deposit composition, other liabilities, management, and personnel including compensation, material contracts, and insurance coverage as well as the branch and facilities information.

The 11 had two weeks to put together their offers in writing. Five sent written non-binding offers. Three have been thanked for their offers and dismissed, so we're down to the final two offers.

We now have two offers who are very close to one another, and we're trying to get some distance between them. This distance will make the decision somewhat easier to manage and to meet our fiduciary duty of maximizing shareholder value. We have asked each of them to go to the next step in dialing in their offers a bit more.

To do so, they are going to want some other information to be able to see if they have any additional value they can draw from. They are also going to need added time to gather that information and make their assessments. So, they have been requested to send a revised offer within 30 days. And we know time is never our friend, so we have added risk in doing so. The added time gives the potential buyers a chance to revise their offer, but it also gives them a chance to change their mind and back out. There would be reputation risk on the parties if they were to back out, but it was still certainly a risk for us as well.

They are likely going to need much more information at this point about your most valuable asset, your people. They will also be exposing this transaction to more people on their side of the table so they can begin to collaborate on the opportunities the combination will present for the bank to "Do & Become." (Where have we heard that before?)

There likely will be a meeting set up for each potential buyer team to meet your team.

Each meeting will be held off-site, likely in a neutral setting for confidentiality, perhaps in your legal counsel's conference room. It's likely that each meeting will take up most of the day. Make sure to plan for that. The potential buyer will likely include their financial leader (CFO), their senior commercial leader, their senior retail leader, their chief credit officer, their chief operations officer, their human resources director, and their investment bankers.

The other information to be uploaded to the virtual data room will now get much more granular. Top customer relationships, top borrowers, top depositors, concentrations, benefit plans, are items likely to be on their list. They will be asking for deeper details.

For each of the people they are bringing to the meeting, there are going to be deeper dive questions for each of their respective areas. That will require you to be represented by the people on your own team who can field those questions. Your inclination will still be to limit the number of people on your end to keep all this confidential.

You still do not have a deal.

Time is not your friend.

If this does get out, your customers instantly move to the top of your competitors' calling lists and your employees will instantly start fielding calls about new opportunities, all of which would be damaging to the value of your bank.

So, you must add your people sparingly. Hopefully, additions will be somebody who has a CIC in place to understand they are in alignment with the project, but that may not always be the case. Additionally, you will want to consider using an Insider Agreement here too, and it's a must-have if you have been using them up to this point.

I am not a lawyer, so it is strongly recommended that you seek legal counsel on your CICs or Insider Agreements.

CHAPTER 23

MANAGEMENT MEETINGS

E ach management meeting is going to be unique to the buyer's strategies, the team they bring to the meeting, and their unique considerations, which could include concerns like this:

- They have a very small market presence and are looking for your bank to essentially carry on as-is, just eliminating or downsizing the back-office duplication (such as accounting, human resources, IT, facilities management, etc.). This would go in tandem with their desire to rely more heavily on the home office for the bulk of the work.

- They may have a market presence already and are primarily interested in the business and market share gains they will have along with the opportunity for growth within that existing customer base. In this case, they would be interested in discerning whether there is (or could be) cannibalization of their existing customer base.

- They may have a line of business that you currently don't have, such as residential construction lending. You could, in this case, bring a new market opportunity for them that works with their residential construction loan operations team, bringing more efficiencies and fee income opportunities to the table. Or, they could add residential mortgages, if you haven't had those capabilities internally before—again, adding market share or additional fee income and consumer deposit accounts.

- It may be that your niche helps them dial in the focus across their organization, such as treasury services, adding more fee income opportunities and market share on the deposit side.

- It could be that your management team aids in their succession planning, which would save them time and possibly money that would otherwise be reserved for finding, recruiting, hiring, and developing leadership.

- It could just be a pure mass play. They get larger, allowing them to continue to make larger and larger acquisitions to fit their strategy.

- Any other considerations related to wealth management, insurance, trust services, added fee income, new lines of business to spread across their footprint, and so forth.

The reasons are limited only by your imagination.

The key is to continue doing as much research on the potential buyers as you can. I know that can be difficult—you are focused on your side of the equation and running the bank, I get that. But it is important for you to look at the opportunity through their eyes, even though they have likely not shared any strategy with you (because they may not win, and don't want that information out there. Even if they do win, they still may not want you to know their strategy, especially if you aren't a part of their longer-term plans because they already have the person who does what you do in place.).

Anticipate what the meeting could be like. Listen to their questions to hypothesize where they may be going with things, then highlight those areas going forward. In essence, figure out what you can do to help add to the picture of what they want to Do—and who they can Become—when the combination takes place.

Have a preparatory meeting with your deal team prior to the management meeting with each potential buyer. *Emphasize to them that you do not have any insight into the buyer's strategy, but that you have a few educated guesses as to what they think may make a powerful combination.* Then go through your thoughts about what that might be and how you can achieve it.

Stress again before adjourning, *this is not confirmed; it is for planning purposes only so they can be aware of where the questions may be heading.*

Remind your team that this is not an interview—we're not that far yet. They will have more time for that down the road.

This is about the bank, what the team has built collectively. The bank is bigger than any one individual in the room. The conversations here are very similar to the conversations we have with examiners: truthful and direct, focused on answering the questions asked.

The buyers want to hear from the team you are bringing. Let them. Allow your team to answer the questions in more detail that are being asked, and only add your comments sparingly and when necessary.

Each buyer's team may also want to meet with your deal team members individually, aligning their team members with your team members by areas of specialty. There may be meetings taking place at the same time, so make sure your team feels confident in their ability to answer questions without you in the room.

If you are the one person that needs to answer all the questions, that will negatively affect how they see your team. If you need time to change your organization so that is not the case, it may be in your best interests to do so. That depends on your individual circumstances and should be well ahead, sometimes by several years, of going down the path of selling the bank.

Following the management meeting, it would be a good idea to consider pulling your deal team together for a debriefing. I urge you to do this as soon as possible following the dismissal of the buyer's team—ideally, on the same day. You will want to compare notes as a team before each of the individual team members have one-on-one conversations about the meeting. Those conversations can bias the information.

Hopefully your investment banker can, and wholeheartedly wants to, sit in. They have had numerous conversations with the leadership of the potential buyer—not only in this transaction, but perhaps on other transactions as well—and could provide great insight…*following* the team debrief. Just like avoiding one-on-one conversations, you don't want the investment banker's perspective to bias the team before they report.

All of this is exhausting, but it is very necessary.

Rinse and repeat for each set of management meetings.

IMPORTANT NOTE: Prior to each management meeting, you will have a meeting with perhaps the CEO of the potential buyer, or the CEO and their investment banker (there may be others, but regardless, this will be a very small group). That meeting may precede the management team meeting, or it may be a week or so in advance of the management meeting. It is often over lunch. Pleasantries, a general probing of how things are going, and the sharing of other thoughts will take place, but the real purpose of the meeting—aside from anything sensational—will be to talk about your team, individually. That may be directly stated from the outset, or it may be more indirect.

The potential buyers are trying to learn who the most critical employees are to the continued earnings of the bank. There will be a great deal of questions about the customer-facing employees, those who have direct interaction with the bank's customers, because the buyer has the back-office functions, those employees who are very important to the ongoing operations of the bank, but don't interact with customers directly, and the buyer will be primarily concerned with keeping customer relationships intact. They will be focusing on each of the employee's backgrounds, their career desires, and your thoughts as to whether they will likely be leaning into the combination and excited about the future.

You have completed a management succession plan—you likely do so annually—and you know this conversation. You have almost certainly already had it in your own mind. Think about that conversation today—where are the weaknesses? What are the areas of most risk that keep you up at night? If it is customer-facing, they will likely arrive at the same conclusion. If it is operational, but with a heavy emphasis of support for your key lines of business, again, they will likely come to the same conclusion. If you have time to correct that prior to going down the sales path, you may want to consider doing so at your earliest convenience. It will come to the surface. It will likely impact value.

This is another point in which they will figure out if you work "on" the business or "in" the business as we discussed in Chapter 9 – Talent.

The management meetings will serve to confirm (or put into question) what you have shared with the members of the deal team. They will likely make judgements on your comments of others, based upon the affirmation they receive back from the conversations with your deal team members.

Let's turn our attention now to the results of the management meetings.

CHAPTER 24

OFFER SUBMISSIONS AND BOARD REVIEW

L ike the deadline for the first set of offers, when the deadline arrives for this set of offers, there is time needed for the investment bankers to deconstruct them to supply a side-by-side comparison. The time is much shorter for this round, however, because there are fewer offers and there are generally not wholesale changes being made. The changes are more select.

Ideally, with all the other information and the added opportunity to gain experience about the "people side" of the business and finer points about customer relationships, concentrations, contracts, and opportunity, both offers would rise. That is the best-case scenario.

There is also the possibility that something is discovered during the process that causes a party to lower their offer. Perhaps they had ideas about the management team that were different from what they discovered during the management meetings. Possibly a realization of credit concentration was discovered in an industry or of a certain product type was discovered that was out-of-favor with the buyer. Or perhaps there was a shareholder with a significant deposit concentration that they would be concerned about leaving once the deal closed.

Equally as likely, they may just affirm the price and terms they have previously offered and are standing firm. If both parties were to stand firm with their existing offers, that would be okay. It would then just add complexity to the decision-making process and bring things such as social considerations, roles for management, and severance (for those without CICs and Stay-Puts), and possibly branding. There also could be the potential for one offer to go up and the other offer to stay the same, as well as for one offer to be pulled and the other offer to stay the same or increase.

So, waiting for this round of offers to come can create anxiety.

There's nothing you can do about it. It is out of your hands, so it's best to continue to carry on as if this may never happen. I know, easier said than done. Again, I went back to that visualization of the decisions being made and having to defend them given the fact the deal didn't happen. Having conscience be your guide is a good plan.

Once the offers arrive and are interpreted by the investment bankers, it is time to pull the board together again for review, analysis, and discussion.

Like the last set of offers, these offers remain non-binding.

If there is opportunity, based on the offers and based on the board's desire to fine tune a point or two, there may be one last request for "best and final" offers or "sharpening their pencil."

Nerve-racking and nail biting. Let's move on to the next chapter to see how to sharpen the pencil.

CHAPTER 25

SHARPENING THE PENCIL

By now, tensions are mounting on all sides.

As was mentioned previously, the end goal is to arrive at the point where there is a willing buyer, a willing seller, and a set of terms that all can agree on. Generally, when all three are present, it's a good time to sell.

So, if there is one more approach to those making offers, it should be worth the risk of asking.

Is what is being asked for a deal-killer? Meaning if the party making a particular request doesn't get the result they were looking for, the whole deal is called off. Or, if you make a particular request, it just puts the buyer off to the point where they pull their offer. You often don't know this in advance—whether this one request will cause them to pull their offer—so there is a fair amount of risk here.

Is what is being asked for, if granted, going to get the deal done? As a seller, you must make certain that what you're asking for is the real reason you are asking for it. Not some reason that you believe the request will not be granted so you can back out and not be seen as the reason the offer didn't come together. With the board involved, the chance of this happening goes down, but it should still be examined. If they grant this request, are we <u>committed</u> to moving forward?

The board needs to consider this.

Is there enough grace with the buyer left for the seller to make the request, and if the answer is no, can the deal still be agreed to?

Will there be long-lasting regret in not asking?

Your natural inclination will be to want to just agree with the given offer and get the deal done and over with, but you must resist the temptation to take the easy path. It's your fiduciary duty.

<u>The strongest leverage you have, as a seller, is at this point in the process. Your leverage will never be higher than at this point.</u>

Once the letter of intent (LOI) is signed your leverage goes away.

You will likely hear from the buyer's side, "It's non-binding, it doesn't matter, you can change it later." It is non-binding but once it is put in writing, it is really hard to get any changes.

If there is an issue that needs to be addressed, it needs to be addressed here.

Suppose one of the terms is an equation that could lower the price before closing and there is no floor on how low the price can go. You may need to consider asking for a floor on the price. With the ability to walk from the deal if the price falls below the floor. You could still opt to close, conditions may have reached a point in the industry or economy where you still want to close, but you have the option of walking as well. This would be an example of the "fiduciary out" that was discussed in Chapter 11 – Shareholders.

You are going to be approaching your shareholders with a price, a price that is subject to risk between the announcement and closing, but even if you explain the "subject to," they will likely only hear the price.

How will it go with your shareholders? Remember. These are friends, family, and people you have life-long relationships with and who you will interact with for the rest of your life.

You need the shareholders' vote to get the deal done.

I am putting these hypotheticals forward to supply a sense of the types of issues that could arise and the underlying related color.

If the other side says all is off, they have "deal fatigue," or they can't see working with you on a going forward basis because this has just taken too much of a toll, are you okay with that answer? If you aren't okay with the answer, and feel there is a possibility this could happen, you (and the board) really need to examine whether you make the request.

No easy answers here.

You will want to plan this out with your investment bankers and your board ahead of time. Think through a roleplay of how the conversation may go with each party. The process of doing so will stimulate thought and conversation.

That conversation will guide your decision-making process in the days to come.

It will prepare your investment bankers for the conversations that might take place by hearing what the priorities are and how the board feels about the level of pushing on the items still waiting to be discussed.

The conversations will likely be different between the parties as the issues with each offer will be different.

One party may need to raise the price and that's it.

You may be asking the other party to raise the price and change some of the terms.

The board conversation will naturally run through what the possible combinations of answers are and can supply direction for the investment banker to position their conversation.

So, the board will likely supply directions for the scenario where the price doesn't move, but the terms change in your favor.

Another scenario would be if one party raises the price and separates from the other.

Another scenario is that the terms get better for the seller.

Another scenario is that the terms get better for the seller *and* the price increases.

Another scenario is neither party move from their current position.

You can see the benefit of going through this process and the dynamics of each scenario aids in pointing out the priorities.

These are tough decisions, but it's important you understand this. You have invested a great deal to get to this point. You cannot take the risk of having communication amongst your board and with your investment bankers be less than clear.

Let's look at what the "best & final" offers look like in the next chapter.

CHAPTER 26

"BEST & FINAL" OFFERS SUBMITTED AND BOARD REVIEW

The deadline has arrived for the "Best & Final" offers. Your investment banker was ready for the conversations and has the answers you have been waiting for. It's time to call the board together again for the conversation.

You have your answers back. You have a party that has separated from the other.

It looks like you have your answer.

The party raised their offer and supplied suggested changes that they would be willing to make to the terms.

The board goes through the terms, and for illustrative purposes, let's say you asked for four changes, and they have agreed to two of them but not to the other two.

There might be an opportunity to take one last bite at the apple.

That's a conversation between the board and the investment banker. If the investment banker believes there is still enough grace to make the ask, the board will need to decide if they would like to take the risk.

The investment banker may recommend against it based on the conversations that have taken place up to that point as well. The investment bankers, on both sides, serve as a buffer between you as the seller and the other side as the buyer. Between the two investment bankers, there can be a reading of their client that gives them insight as to when they have reached a boiling point. It's another great reason to engage investment bankers.

You likely have everything you have been looking for now. You have a willing seller, you have a willing buyer, and a set of terms that you can all agree upon.

Congratulations, that's a good time to sell!

But don't celebrate yet, we've got to get this into a Letter of Intent (LOI), let's move to the next chapter.

CHAPTER 27

LETTER OF INTENT (LOI) AND BOARD APPROVAL

Your investment banker has had a conversation with the investment banker of the buyer. We have a deal, verbally.

That means it's time to at least put the offer in writing through the Letter of Intent (LOI). However, even in writing it remains a non-binding offer.

Also, do not be surprised if you haven't heard directly from your counterpart on the buying side.

There is work to do before we get to closing and that conversation will take place a bit later.

For perspective, we reached this point seven months after the board's decision to explore strategic options and ultimately pursue a possible sale.

There is still a high degree of risk between now and when the "definitive agreement" (or merger agreement) is signed, and we will be covering that process from now through Chapter 32 – Communication of the Transaction.

The Letter of Intent (LOI) spells out the details of the <u>framework</u> of what is going to be worked on in greater detail in the definitive agreement.

If you follow golf, you'll know that when word broke of the merger between the PGA and the LIV golf tour, it was a nightmare for the PGA director. The media and the players are wanting answers as to how the new merger will work and there were none.

This is a real-world example of why you don't want any word out about the merger prior to having the definitive agreement negotiated and agreed to. The announcement led to pure chaos, and every stakeholder was weighing in as to how this will all work. This was a no-win situation. I cannot imagine negotiating the definitive agreement under these conditions. It will be a case study for business classes.

The LOI is still non-binding. It is the framework of the agreement, the details of which you are about to negotiate. You are now focused on working with this one party to see this through. *For a copy of a fictitious LOI, please go to www.KurtKnutson.com/BonusContent.*

The investment bankers will review the terms to ensure they are what has been agreed to up to this point. If both sides are using an investment banker, the chance there is something that is misunderstood is very low. I'm not saying the odds are zero, but the likelihood of their being a major misunderstanding is very low. They will supply their review to the board and the LOI will be subject to board approval. Your corporate documents and by-laws will govern the vote required to approve. Regardless of what is required, it is everybody's goal to have the board voting 100% for approval. This is the last look at all the terms and conditions prior to signing, and when signed, it serves as the framework document for the definitive agreement.

This is a major accomplishment. Congratulate yourself for getting to this point. Just don't let the congratulations go to your head. After all, there is still a great deal of work to do.

Your legal counsel really hasn't been too involved up to this point and that's all about to change.

Let's get to it.

Turn to the next chapter to learn all about the definitive agreement and the process involved.

CHAPTER 28

DEFINITIVE AGREEMENT & DISCLOSURE SCHEDULES

The definitive agreement is the terms and conditions along with the representations and warranties and various other details of the merger.

Once the definitive agreement is completed and signed, _then_ the agreement to merge is announced.

As has been pointed out several times during the description of the process, time is not your friend.

This is where experienced bank M&A legal counsel is prized. Ideally, both the buyer and the seller have experienced legal counsel with significant M&A deal experience. Anything short of that will likely lead to inefficiencies, both in the deal itself and your time management. It's too important to try to use somebody without significant deal experience.

The negotiation and completion of the definitive agreement can be a considerably long and drawn-out process, especially if legal counsel lacks experience and repetition. Ensure that at least the lead counsel on your legal team has several successfully closed transactions in their past. Even for experienced lawyers, if the buyer and seller (particularly the seller) don't push for expediting the process, the starting and stopping along the way may take more time than it should.

I liken this process to a real estate development project. You can have experienced civil engineers, experienced architects, and an experienced general contractor, each of which does impeccable work. But the developer organizes them and pays attention to the deadlines for having everything into the city for approval keeping the project on time. The developer starts from the end date and works backwards to today to get everything tracking towards that end date. Time is not your friend, so play the role of the developer in negotiating that the definitive agreement gets done on time (**please note**: the negotiation needs to happen with the LOI negotiations and be included in the LOI).

Push for the definitive agreement to be completed in as little as 30 days. As the seller, this should be a point of negotiation and included in the LOI.

As a reader of this book, you have the advantage of having this information, so make a note of it to ensure that it is included in your terms.

The lawyers on both sides will likely appreciate the short time frame because it does keep everybody focused. Experienced lawyers, with bank M&A repetition, will be able to focus on the issues that aren't necessary for you to be involved in. If your involvement is needed, they will let you know. They will also report to you anything that is out of the ordinary and where they would like your approval prior to proceeding.

This allows you to focus on the things that will require a great deal of your attention, namely the covenants and the representations and warranties. You will also be preparing the proxy materials for the shareholders' meeting and, oh, by the way, managing the bank.

Prior to getting into the definitive agreement, your lawyers will likely provide you with a list of the items needed for the disclosure schedules. The disclosure schedules are the supporting documentation for the covenants and representations and warranties. The descriptions of the documents in the disclosure schedules are summaries of the specific terms of the documents they reference.

So, there are a whole host of documents that need to be gathered, and the lawyers are supplying the list so the gathering process can begin. The most burdensome of the documents are benefit plan documents and "material contracts." In short, "material contracts" are anything larger than an agreed upon amount, say $25,000. All benefit plan documents will be important because the buyer will most likely be replacing them with their own and will need to be checked for regulatory compliance.

TIP: *Here is a tip that could be of great help to you if you could be contemplating a sale, now or further out into the future. Make both items, benefits plan documents, and material contracts (I would even go as low as $10,000 for a fuller view) a part of an annual vendor management program review with your board. Gathering these documents can be a head scratcher for all involved employees and could raise suspicions. If it was a part of your annual vendor management program review process with the board, it is never more than 11 months old during a sale and doesn't disrupt anybody.*

(This is for illustration purposes only. Please keep in mind that I am not a lawyer, and this is by no means a replacement for seeking legal counsel. I would highly encourage you to do such.)

In summary, here is what a definitive agreement may include:

Merger Structure – Details of the mechanics of the merging of the various entities and the effective date of the merger.

Treatment of the Company Common Stock – Details the price per share the holders of the stock will receive in a cash deal, or the number of shares exchanged in a stock deal, and both in a cash/stock combination deal, and any details of what may impact that price per share or exchange rate (or both) between the signing of the definitive agreement and the closing.

Procedure for Exchange of the Stock Certificates – Details the timing and method for exchanging the shares for cash, stock, or both depending on the deal. You are likely to receive calls and emails once the deal is announced—prior to proxy materials being sent to shareholders—asking who they need to send their stock certificates to and when they will get their cash. Be prepared for that.

Representations and Warranties – Detailed representations and warranties on behalf of both the buyer and seller to things such as:

- Organization, corporate standing, qualification to do business and corporate power.

- Authorization of the definitive agreement and the merger.

- Execution, performance and delivery of the definitive agreement will not conflict with, or violate, any organizational documents or certain material contracts.

- Filing of regulatory reports and statements.

- Absence of certain adverse changes or events.

- Compliance with laws and regulations.

The seller will likely make additional representations and warranties related to:

- Financial and tax matters.

- Legal and regulatory matters.

- Ownership of real property and insurance coverage.

- Lending and loan matters.

- Investments and securities matters.

- Contracts and conduct of business.

- Compliance with environmental laws.

- Intellectual property matters.

- Employee matters, labor matters and employee benefit plans.

- Transactions with affiliates.

- Broker's fees.

- Fiduciary accounts and investment activities.

The buyer will likely make additional representations and warranties as to:

- The ability to come up with the cash in an all-cash transaction.

- Similar representations and warranties as the seller for a stock or partial stock transaction.

Conduct of the Business of the Seller Pending the Merger – Customary covenants on the operation of the business prior to the closing of the merger. Under the covenants, it is generally anticipated that the seller follows the ordinary course of business, consistent with past practice. Covenants such as these generally place restrictions on certain activities that the seller may enter into without consent of the buyer, including but not limited to the following items:

- Issuing any added shares of stock or creating new stock awards or grants under benefit plans.

- Declaring or paying dividends on the stock.

- Entering into, amending or renewing any material contract.

- Extending new credit to any person that would exceed a mutually agreed upon dollar amount.

- Maintaining the allowance for loan and lease losses at a certain dollar level or failing to charge-off any loan that would be deemed uncollectible under GAAP.

- Selling, transferring, or otherwise encumbering any assets, properties, deposits, or business subject to certain exceptions provided for in the definitive agreement.

- Buying all or any part of the assets, deposits, properties, or business of any other entity.

- Amending the organizational documents.

- Implementing or adopting any change in accounting principles, practices, or methods other than what is required by GAAP.

- Increasing compensation or benefits of any current or former director, officer, or employee or accelerating vesting of any stock-based compensation or any other long-term incentive compensation.

- Establishing, amending, or becoming a party to any stock option plan or other stock-based compensation plan or other employee benefit.

- Incurring or guaranteeing any indebtedness other than in the ordinary course of business.

- Entering into any new line of business.

- Materially changing and lending, investment, underwriting, risk and asset liability management or other banking and operation policies.

- Settling any action, claim, suit, or going ahead for an amount in excess of an agreed upon amount.

- Opening, moving, or closing any branch.

- Entering into an employment or similar agreement.

In general, the seller agrees to use its best efforts to preserve its business organization and assets and to keep its rights and customer relationships as well.

No Solicitation of Acquisition Proposals – The seller agrees not to directly or indirectly ask for or encourage any other acquisition proposals. If the seller receives an unsolicited bona fide proposal that the seller, in good faith, believes to be superior to the terms of the definitive agreement, the seller may take part in discussions related to the superior proposal. There is also an agreement that the seller has asked its advisors or other representatives not to engage in any of the activities.

Employee Benefits – Generally, the terms of employment, compensation, bonuses, benefits, severance, CICs, Stay-Puts, etc., and post-closing are addressed here.

Conditions to Consummation of the Merger – Various conditions for both parties generally include but are not limited to items such as:

- Accuracy of each party's respective representations and warranties.

- Performance and compliance in all material respects with the obligations of the definitive agreement.

- Receipt of all regulatory approvals.

- Receipt of approval from the seller's shareholders.

- The absence of legal proceedings, injunctions, or restraints that would prevent the merger, or would cause it to be illegal.

- Receipt by each party of an officer's certificate from the other party certifying as to certain matters of the merger.

Termination of the Definitive Agreement – Generally, the merger may be ended by the parties under the following circumstances, among others:

- Mutual consent of the buyer and seller.

- By either buyer or seller in the event of a material breach under the definitive agreement which cannot be cured within a mutually agreed upon cure period (e.g., 30 days) after written notice has been provided to the breaching party (provided the party seeking the termination is not already in material breach of the definitive agreement).

- By either buyer or seller if the regulatory approval of the merger is denied or if there has been a request to withdraw the application by the regulators.

- By either the buyer or seller if the seller's shareholder approval is not obtained.

- By either the buyer or the seller if the merger has not happened by an agreed upon date (through no fault of the party looking to end).

- By either buyer or seller if any court or regulatory authority issues a judgment, order, injunction or takes any other action restraining, enjoining, or otherwise prohibiting the merger.

- By the buyer if the seller does not recommend the merger for approval by the shareholders.

- By the seller if they enter into a proposal with terms superior to the terms of the definitive agreement.

Payment Upon Termination – The seller would have to pay the buyer an agreed upon termination payment if any of the following were to take place:

- Buyer terminates the merger due to the seller's material breach of its obligation to call a shareholder's meeting and recommend that the shareholders vote in favor of the merger.

- The buyer terminates the merger because the seller is soliciting or encouraging negotiations or discussions relating to an acquisition proposal.

- Buyer terminates the merger because the seller is proposing to withhold, withdraw, qualify or adversely modify its recommendation to the shareholders to vote in favor of approval of the merger.

- The seller terminates the merger because it has accepted an unsolicited proposal with terms superior to the terms of the definitive agreement.

Waiver and Amendment – Generally, the definitive agreement can be amended by both parties, but once the shareholder vote has been held and approved, essentially any amendments following will require approval of the shareholders. Again, the level of votes "for" will be spelled out in your corporate documents. Your goal, however, should be to get that approval number as high as possible so you reduce the likelihood of a shareholder, or shareholders, objecting to the sale and holding things up. Your legal counsel will be providing guidance here.

Expenses – Addresses which expenses, including but not limited to fees and expenses of their own counsel and accountants the buyer and seller handle. Legal and professional expenses incurred by any shareholder in connection with the merger for any related documents are the responsibility of the individual shareholder.

Effect of Merger on the Rights of Company Shareholders – At the time of the closing of the merger, holders of the shares of the buyer will cease to have any rights (in the case of a cash sale) and will only have the right to receive their share of the merger consideration as spelled out in the definitive agreement. In the case of a partial combination cash and stock sale or an all-stock sale, your shareholders will become shareholders of the buyer and will likely need to sign the buyer's shareholders agreement. Those provisions will be spelled out here as well.

Voting Agreements and Restrictive Covenant Agreements – The directors and executive officer of the seller will enter into voting agreements, agreeing to vote in favor of the merger. The directors and executive officer of the seller will also have entered into restrictive covenant agreements whereby they have agreed to covenants that likely include, but are not limited to, the following:

- Not to solicit former officers or employees for an agreed upon period.

- Not to compete for an agreed upon period of time, likely within an agreed upon certain geographic area.

Another item you will likely want to add to the LOI during the negotiation process is directors & officers (D&O) insurance coverage for a period of six years beyond the closing, to be paid by the buyer (if possible). This provides coverage for the unlikely event of a lawsuit brought against the seller for actions prior to the merger. Good protection to have for both the seller and the buyer.

<u>As a reader of this book, you have the advantage of having this information too, so make a note of it to ensure that it is included in your terms</u>.

As you can see, getting the definitive agreement to a point of signing in 30 days is going to be a tall order. And yes, you still need to manage the bank. Let's look at some additional considerations there in the next chapter.

CHAPTER 29

REVERSE DUE DILIGENCE

While hammering out the details of the definitive agreement and gathering all the information necessary for the buyer's due diligence, the seller has due diligence to address as well. In our case, it was quite simple, because we were selling for cash. So, our primary interests were in whether the buyer could come up with the cash at closing, and whether there would be anything that could stand in the way of regulatory approval (we'll talk about that in Chapter 36 – Regulatory Approval).

But if you are selling for merger consideration for stock or a cash and stock combination, the reverse due diligence process gets more involved. It has been mentioned on a few occasions in this book that future plans aren't often shared with the seller in an all-cash transaction, particularly until the definitive agreement is signed. That's understandable, because until the definitive agreement is signed, this is still a non-binding offer. Even after the definitive agreement is signed, there is always the possibility that the deal does not close.

Reverse due diligence in this case refers to an analysis performed on the buyer. Analyzing the ability to close on the transaction and if they are suitable partners/ investors/buyers. Just as potential buyers conduct careful evaluation of the seller's operations, it is important to perform the same evaluation of the buyer to a varying degree related to the amount of future execution risk leftover for the seller's shareholders following the closing of the deal. If the seller's shareholders are receiving a portion of their merger consideration in stock as in a cash and stock deal or all of it in stock in an all-stock deal, they are then subject to the buyer's ability to maintain value or increase it going forward. As such, the purchase price should be greater than an all-cash price because of the time value of money. The extent of due diligence on the buyer is higher when there is an all-stock or partial stock deal because the risk is greater over time compared to an all-cash deal today.

There should be an equally extensive evaluation of the buyer in an all-stock deal because all the value is tied to the future performance of the buyer's stock, so there is a substantial amount of execution risk to the seller's shareholders. There would need to be extensive sharing of plans between buyer and seller as well as possibly key management roles and board seats that should be in play. The confidentiality risk is the same as it was prior to this. It's just the buyer's willingness to share that "future" information, plans and strategies.

When comparing two hypothetical buyers' offers with one being all-cash and the other being a cash and stock combination or all-stock, the combination or all-stock offer should be significantly higher than the all-cash offer to offset the execution risk being assumed by the seller's shareholders.

In the investment banking world, reverse due diligence can carry two meanings. One being where a company performs due diligence on itself to assess its readiness for sale before being presented to prospective buyers. This "self" due diligence is usually performed by a third party on behalf of the company. Without the third-party aspect, Section 1 of this book is essentially that type of reverse due diligence.

The other meaning is what was referenced above, an analysis performed on the buyer. This is what is being applied at this point in the transaction, following the execution of the LOI and during the process of negotiating the definitive agreement, prior to an announcement. The last thing any seller wants is to announce a deal and the buyer can't get it done.

At minimum, an evaluation of the buyer's ability to close should be done. Do they have a history of having successfully made acquisitions in the past? Can they come up with the cash merger consideration necessary, if applicable? What is their relationship with their primary regulator? Do they have adequate capital before and after they make the acquisition?

As stock comes into play with the buyer's offer, then what is the quality of their earnings? The quality of their assets? Have you seen projections? What are the assumptions they are basing the projections on? Are they using the purchase of your bank as an interim step to gain critical mass to make another acquisition(s)? Are they trying to reach a certain asset level to then sell to an even larger bank? If so, what are the buyer's desires or assumptions on that sale – cash merger proceeds or stock or a combination? These are just a sample of the types of questions that should be asked and are used to stimulate thought.

Selling to a bank who, in turn, wants to gain the scale to sell to another bank can be an attractive option for your shareholders but does come with execution risk that should undergo a level evaluation commensurate to the risk. In other words, you sell your bank to another bank and take all-stock as merger consideration. One to three years later they sell their bank. The general thought goes that you essentially have sold your bank twice. This happened in the frothier bank M&A world of the mid-1990's and there were some very happy shareholders as a result. A change in interstate banking laws made that environment a bit more predictable at the time. In today's world, there would be a substantial amount of additional risk in my opinion. But does occasionally take place.

There is always something else that should be considered. Let's check out a few more topics of note.

CHAPTER 30

MANAGING THE BANK

T he level of inquiry goes up substantially throughout this process. The deal team manages the process throughout. There is periodic involvement of the investment bankers during this part of the process, but the lion's share of the work at this point is between the deal team and legal counsel. Documents for this part of the process are generally shared directly with legal counsel, who in turn gathers them and forwards them in coordination with the buyer's counsel.

Parallel to working on the definitive agreement and the disclosure schedules, you will begin working on the proxy materials (the materials are detailed in Chapter 35 – Shareholder Meeting) for the shareholder's meeting and going through the mechanics of the conversion of your shares at closing (this is discussed further in Chapter 41 – Conversion of Shares). Suffice it to say, as soon as the announcement of the merger is made (following the signing of the definitive agreement), the shareholders' first questions will be, "When do I get my money (or stock, or cash and stock)?" followed by, "How does the process work?"

You and members of the deal team will be answering questions, gathering documentation, and responding to requests from your legal counsel very frequently over the time chosen to get the definitive agreement done. Again, I would recommend 30 days from the signing date of the LOI, if possible, as time is not your friend. The LOI is just a framework of the agreement to merge. The definitive agreement is the framework spelled out in detail as to the mechanics of how the merger will work along with representations and warranties of both the buyer and the seller. The 30 days is largely for gathering all the supporting documents for the representations and warranties. All of those supporting documents will need to be reviewed by the buyer and could possibly bring something to light that could delay or cause the whole merger to derail.

There's no way of putting a pretty bow on this—this part of the process is truly a grind.

You, the board, and the deal team are still the only ones with knowledge of the transaction. Board approval of the definitive agreement is upcoming within a few days of completing the definitive agreement, followed by an announcement of the merger to customers, employees, shareholders, and the media.

You still have a bank to run, albeit with some new constraints to be mindful of as pointed out in Chapter 28 – Definitive Agreement & Disclosure Schedules. They are not committed fully to writing yet, but they need to be treated that way in principle so as not to put anything in jeopardy right out of the gate. That does have to be balanced with the fact that this transaction is not done by any means. A nuclear war could break out, derailing it, and if that sounds too far-fetched, we'll make it a global pandemic instead. That should help keep it feeling real.

At this point, the only thing we can hang our hat on is a non-binding LOI. If the transaction doesn't move forward, the bank needs to keep moving forward without it. That needs to be remembered.

Decisions you would make daily if there were no deal happening still need to take place, now those decisions must be passed through a lens. You're one of a few people that know about the lens, so you need to adjust accordingly. The loan approval process is one big lens you need to be concerned with as well as any major decisions going forward. When in doubt about whether a decision violates a covenant or changes the complexion of the transaction, discuss it with your legal counsel.

Make sure to keep in mind if things go the wrong direction, you are ultimately accountable. It's a great deal of pressure. You need to ensure the bank continues to perform, if something were to happen like a large borrower suddenly announces difficulties that put the repayment of their debt in jeopardy, or you suffer a major cybersecurity event, or a key employee decides to leave for an opportunity elsewhere, these could change the value, terms, or possibly derail the whole sale. Another possibility is the supporting documentation for the representations and warranties contradicts what you have recollected. Now doubt is placed in the buyer's mind about a few issues and your credibility is damaged.

Do your own thinking and embrace the grind. The best advice I can provide is to break your tasks down into smaller pieces and keep focused on completing the next one. Then the next one after that. The old axiom of "What's the best way to eat an elephant? One bite at a time" holds true.

Once the grind is complete, it's time to bring the board back into the picture. We'll cover that in the next chapter.

BOARD APPROVAL

Y ou have made it through and embraced the grind.

The definitive agreement has made it to final form and is ready for board approval.

The bank continues to perform well.

The time to announce the deal is right around the corner.

Your mind is racing with thoughts about what the shareholders will think, what the employees will think, and what the customers will think.

What will the next few months hold prior to closing?

What could possibly happen that could derail closing?

Will the regulators approve the deal? How long will that take?

You haven't had an opportunity to think about what your role will be going forward. Unfortunately, that will continue to take a back seat.

For now, you must just focus on the step directly in front of you. Board approval.

As with all the board meetings on this topic, the special meeting is limited to just the directors. In addition to the board, the investment bankers and legal counsel attend as well.

In our case, and for your time reference, this meeting took place seven months past our first meeting on the topic. We were pretty much right on the date in the deal timeline that had originally been presented to the board by the investment bankers.

Legal counsel will typically remind the directors of their duties, which were outlined in Chapter 11 – Shareholders. The duties of good faith, care, and loyalty; take a moment to flip back and reread the chapter if you need a refresher. Legal counsel will answer any questions that may have arisen during the review process. Questions like, "In your opinion, did you see anything that you perceived as acting in self-interest come into play with our decision to go with this buyer?" Or "Do you feel, given your background and experience, that this process ultimately achieved the best outcome for the shareholders?"

If you have engaged the investment bankers to supply a fairness opinion, which documents the process followed by the board during the sale to mitigate risk of shareholder liability, the investment bankers will walk the board through a summary of the fairness opinion. The summary is a high-level review of the very detailed financial analysis they have carried out to arrive at their conclusion. Following the walkthrough of their analysis, they will issue their opinion as to whether the merger consideration to be received by the shareholders is fair from a financial point of view. The investment bankers will answer any questions that may have arisen during the fairness opinion process.

Next, legal counsel will provide a summary overview of the definitive agreement, voting rights, and restrictive covenants. As you can imagine, despite this being a summary, it can take some time. The directors are encouraged to ask questions throughout the entire review process.

Following those items, a brief description of the timeline of the remaining process is discussed.

What is left to finish, generally, is:

- Approving your side of the transaction and executing the signature pages to be held in escrow by your counsel.

- The buyer's board approves their side of the transaction and executes the signature pages to be held in escrow by their counsel.

- Announcing the buyer and seller have signed a definitive agreement to merge.

- Continuous work by both sides on various closing matters (we will cover in Chapter 33 – Closing Checklist).

- A special shareholder meeting of the seller asking for approval of the transaction.

- Obtaining regulatory approval.

- Closing the deal.

- Conversion of the shares for the merger consideration.

And, of course, at the closing your board will cease to exist as the bank and the holding company (if applicable) will cease to exist.

There may be members of your board, or all of your board, continuing with the merged bank/holding company if there was a stock or cash and stock combination for merger consideration. In an all-cash transaction, there are likely no members of your board moving on with the merged bank/holding company board(s).

The board is reminded that the announcement of the signed definitive agreement stays confidential until legal counsel confirms that everything is in order from a documentation perspective. The non-board shareholder to this point still has no knowledge of the deal until it is announced.

Congratulations on reaching this achievement. It is a significant milestone.

Your relationships with customers, employees, and shareholders will be moving to a new chapter and it is too significant not to acknowledge it here.

You have invested a great deal in all those relationships. Now you know how those relationships will be affected in the long term. Your key employees will benefit from the CICs and Stay-Puts (if you have them), they will have a much bigger platform in which to continue their careers, your customers will have more borrowing capacity to grow, more products and more locations will be available, your shareholders will be able to monetize their investment and will have participated in the value creation and the buyer will have great employees and great customers helping build value for their shareholders as well. The community you have served will now be served by a bigger bank with more resources.

There will undoubtedly be some transition noise along the way that may test some of those relationships, but if you've done it the right way, history will be on your side. That noise arises mostly from places you weren't expecting. Perhaps a key employee who may be looking at this emotionally and is upset it is happening. Or perhaps, shareholders who may not have wanted to sell their investment at this time because they were hoping for a longer-term time horizon or are themselves emotionally attached to the investment. I am not saying there will be a tremendous amount of it, but there will likely be something that surprises you.

Things are about to change.

The actual announcement of the signed definitive agreement is the product of collaboration between the buyer and seller and is the topic of the next chapter.

CHAPTER 32

COMMUNICATION OF THE TRANSACTION

Your board has approved the transaction and the buyer will be seeking approval of the transaction from their board as well. The two meetings are typically scheduled very close to one another from a date and time perspective. Once both approvals have taken place, it's now time to share with others.

You're about to announce that you're selling the bank.

The audience for the announcement, for both you and the buyer, consists of the following:

- Management team
- Employees
- Advisory board (if applicable)
- Media
- Customers

This is really the first coordinated effort between the two banks. This is the first step in the process of each party talking about "us" and "them," eventually evolving to just talking about "us."

In a perfect world, the two organizations would have collaborated for a month on the message and the communication plan and would be well-choreographed and ready to roll out that answers everybody's questions in a timely manner. In the real world, however, it just doesn't work that way.

So, what may happen is that about two or three days before the board meetings, there will be a very general conversation between the two parties on how the announcement should take place.

There may be some strict communication requirements you need to incorporate into your planning, such as those that a public company must adhere to. Like after the market closes so filings can be made before the market opens next. If that is the case, those will need to guide the announcement process.

You are knowledgeable about the fact that there is very little time following the finalization of the definitive agreement and board approval, and as soon as board approval happens, an announcement is going to take place. <u>As a reader of this book, you have an advantage. You can work on your message well in advance. The advanced preparation will make you much more comfortable delivering the message.</u>

The message will, however, need to be coordinated with the buyer. They may, or may not, share their message with you but you will likely need to share yours with them for their prior review. The two messages don't have to be exactly alike, as there are two separate organizations talking about the upcoming merger. It's expected to see both a buyer's, and a seller's perspective—still, they should both be positive and generally use the same overarching themes.

Also, keep in mind that you have been aware of a possible transaction and have gone through the process for quite some time now, but this is the first time that the audience has heard about this.

Most people have no idea of the process involved in getting to this point and most people have no idea about the process that comes next. It is their perception that once this announcement is made, a switch gets flipped, signs get changed, and the world starts as if their bank is now a part of another bank. To them, it's as simple as night becoming day.

It is important to understand this view and to work from there.

The best advice I can provide regarding this is to think through the message that your employees, your customers and your shareholders need to hear. Build that message and refine it. Also, as has been mentioned previously, keep in mind that the merger hasn't *officially* happened yet. There are some things that are outside of your control that could delay things or even prevent them from happening. Something that could happen from a big picture perspective that could impact it—another pandemic, for example. Regulatory approval could prevent it from happening. A problem with the seller that presents itself unexpectedly. A problem with the buyer that presents itself unexpectedly. Fraud involving a large borrower could be an example of this.

Prepare for the worst and hope for the best.

The key word is "prepare," which doesn't mean "act."

It is also important to understand that the message needs to be disciplined and not overly expressive about the combination. Keep it business-like. You don't want to make it so expressive that a change in course creates the need to embark on a whole new campaign trying to resurrect your brand as a stand-alone brand.

You will want to communicate how this merger came about. I doesn't mean the process we've covered in this book. What your customers, employees, and shareholders will be most interested in is the answer to this question: "*Why is this happening?*"

Then, they're going to want to know *how this affects them.* And *when is it happening?*

Keep in mind, they have no context, so they think this is happening tomorrow. A flipped switch, remember? You're going to have to set expectations.

What can they expect from the new combination? How will they benefit?

As mentioned previously, your shareholders' first questions are, "*How much is my stock worth?*" And "*When do I get my money?*"

Your employees' first questions are, "*What does this mean for me?*" And "*Do I still have a job?*" And "What will my pay be?"

Your customers' first questions are, "*How does this impact my business?*" and "*Will I still be working with the same people?*" and "*Will the products and services we use still be the same?*"

You're starting to get an outline here.

The timing of your announcement, as previously discussed, will need to be coordinated with the buyer.

You may wish to have a smaller meeting with the management team to prepare them first.

After all, they are going to be getting asked the same questions by their team immediately following the "all-employee" announcement. It will be better to have them in the loop prior to the announcement even if it is two or three hours so they can have some time to begin to digest the news.

If you have CICs and Stay-Put agreements with the team, they will likely be leaning into the announcement as well since they will benefit from the merger. If so, remind them of the confidentiality clause in their CICs and not jeopardize their benefit. Again, emphasize the importance of not letting word get out in advance of the meeting.

Additionally, if you have gotten Insider Agreements from your board and your deal team, it would be wise to have each member of the management team sign one at the start of the meeting, prior to sharing the message. You can explain to them that you have important information you wish to share, but to hear the information, they will need to sign the agreement as each individual board member did.

Allow them time to read it and to ask any questions about the agreement before they voluntarily sign.

I am not a lawyer, so it is strongly recommended that you seek legal counsel on your Insider Agreement.

Later in the day, in the case of a public company buyer, just after the market closes, you will likely hold your "all-employee" meeting. The buyer may wish to attend your meeting, so there will need to be some coordination there. Again, follow the buyer's preference. *But always keep in mind the deal isn't done yet. A savvy and experienced buyer will handle it in this fashion as well.* If you are dealing with a particularly pushy buyer wanting to move beyond your comfort level with the message, ask your team for assistance—your legal counsel and your investment bankers—to get involved in the background. The buyer will likely want to follow your comments with comments of their own. They may wish to see your comments in advance and may not share theirs in advance with you. Just be aware.

The buyer may have others from their bank at the meeting too—likely some department heads, human resources, etc.—to help answer questions employees may have and to let them know they will be meeting with them as time progresses towards closing.

Prior to adjourning the meeting, hand out copies of the press release to all employees, and hand out a pre-prepared frequently asked questions list. The frequently asked questions will be the same talking points from your announcement. It will just be in another format which allows for people to process the information differently. It will give the employees a resource to refer to as they begin to get questions from family and friends during the evening (and some customers too). It will be an aid for them as they arrive the following morning when there is certain to be a great deal of conversation on the topic.

It is likely that while the employee meeting is taking place, a press release, issued by the buyer, has gone out. While you may or may not get an opportunity to see the press release <u>before</u> it goes out, you should get a copy <u>as it goes out</u> from the buyer. Again, if you are having difficulty seeing the press release, ask your team—your legal counsel and the investment bankers—for assistance in the background. The buyer's legal counsel and the investment bankers from both sides will want to see it as well because they will want to be included in it too.

Following the "all-employee" meeting, if you have an advisory board, you may wish to strongly consider inviting them to attend a special meeting. Your advisory board is likely to be your biggest and/or your most influential customers, and they really should be hearing this message from you personally rather than reading about it or hearing about it from a friend or another banker vying for their business. In addition to hearing the news from you, they also have an opportunity to hear from the buyer as the word is hitting the street. It provides an opportunity for immediate introductions to the buyer, which is beneficial to both the advisory board members and the buyer. Provide a copy of the press release and the frequently asked questions to the advisory directors prior to their departure.

You will want to have crafted an email message to your shareholders prior to all the meetings, but that email won't go out until the announcements have been made. The message will be a shareholder-tailored message but should be very similar to the message provided to the employees and should include copies of the press release and the frequently asked questions. You will want to let your shareholders know that they will be receiving more details in the coming weeks. This is a message coming from you. The buyer will want to see an advance copy, typically through sharing with your legal counsel who in turn shares it with the buyer's legal counsel, who in turn shares it with the buyer. So, you will have to build some time into the process to accommodate this going forward.

Side note: *Make your shareholders aware of the fact that they will need to surrender their stock certificate(s) when the deal closes, and one thing they can begin doing immediately is locating their stock certificate(s). This will allow for more time to replace "lost" certificates before it becomes really costly if the paying agent or stock transfer agent has to become involved. Continue to remind shareholders to locate their certificate(s) in subsequent communications.*

The press, customers, or shareholders may try to reach you once the word gets out. The announcement you prepared for the stakeholders we have just gone through are your talking points. Stay disciplined and stay on message. You will have this feeling of a giant weight being lifted off your shoulders because others now know the Big Secret. You're going to be hit with the urge to relax.

Don't.

You have come too far, and this is too important to relax.

There will be time for relaxing later.

You may wish to make posts on social media regarding the announcement that evening. My advice would be that it isn't necessary, there will be more time for that as things move towards closing or post-closing. But social media is ever evolving, and circumstances could change.

You *will* want to update your website with a simple announcement on the homepage with links to a copy of the press release and the frequently asked questions. This will aid your customers as they are logging into online or mobile banking in finding out the news from you and will provide some of the answers they are seeking right away.

Our experience was that people didn't get overly excited about things, many (if not most) read the press release and frequently asked questions sheets and were knowledgeable when they did speak with the team.

We'll get back to managing the bank again in the next chapter. You will find there has been a shift you will need to accommodate for.

SECTION 4

ANNOUNCEMENT TO CLOSING

CHAPTER 33

MANAGING THE BANK

F ollowing the announcement of the signing of the definitive agreement and the upcoming merger, you will notice a subtle emotional shift from your customers and employees. It's normal and to be expected, but it is almost immediate. It can be a bit of a surprise at the swiftness of the shift, but again, when examined from a distance it is entirely normal.

That shift is in the fact that you are now not viewed as the "final word."

Although the merger hasn't officially closed, in a de facto way it has.

It's important to understand, and it is something you'll have to navigate. As has been said many times now, the deal isn't done yet. Until the deal is done, there is always a possibility it may not get done.

You will need to navigate this time in the same spirit as your announcement comments. Respectful, positive, collaborative, and forward-thinking, but with distance as well. The distance is preventative so that a retreat from the position is still workable until the deal is closed.

You're in a tricky position because you may or may not have a role going forward, and you may not know the answer to that question yet. This may or may not have been spelled out in the LOI. Or it may have stated you're still going to be involved but does not address the level or manner in which that will take place. You will be compensated according to the Stay-Put, if one is in place, but that period of time may be shorter than listed. That's okay; that's the buyer's decision and they paid for the right to that decision. The buyer, your potential new employer, may never have been in this position before and may view you as being aloof or not caring about the new organization or disengaged. That isn't the case. By defense, as the leader of your current organization, you must do this—it is part of your fiduciary duties. Your fiduciary duties are not relieved until the shareholders receive their money.

Your team will be meeting with their future leaders and will be leaning towards the future in their words and actions, which is what your team needs to do as well. There likely will be times when they know more about the future direction than you do and that will be very strange since you were always a part of defining the future.

Your team needs to know what the future holds, not only on their own behalf, but on the customers' behalf too. The customers want to know what the future holds. The employees are the eyes and ears of the customers. The employees need to be able to communicate that picture of the future as positively and as clearly as they can.

The buyer ultimately is the only one who can paint that picture. That means it's the buyer's responsibility to provide as clear a picture for the employees as possible. The future is their vision. Not your vision, their vision. If that picture is confusing, it will lead to losing employees and customers. This communication must be the highest priority the buyer has, but sadly, it often isn't. If this is the case, the only advice I can provide is to encourage your team to stay positive. Let them know these things take time, and advocate for them where you are able.

Employees, by reflex, will be looking to you for answers. It is important to communicate those are answers you cannot supply and that you are hopeful they will be supplied soon. The only thing you can do is ask them for faith and patience that the answers will be coming soon. Our number one goal is to make things run as smoothly as possible so that our customers are taken care of. We all need a periodic reminder that if the customers aren't taken care of, we all lose.

This requires understanding, patience, and diplomacy as you continue to grind towards the finish line of getting the merger closed. It could be easy for a leader to disengage during this time. You will feel a sense of loss, which is natural, and it requires being the ultimate professional and seeing things through.

Leaders lead.

Keep your eye on the ball and support the team.

Yes, the definitive agreement is calling. Time to get on the Closing Checklist, which we'll cover in the next chapter.

CHAPTER 34

CLOSING CHECKLIST

O kay, you've hammered out the definitive agreement, announced the signing of the agreement and the upcoming merger to your employees, customers, and shareholders, and you are back to the execution of the definitive agreement.

Back to embracing the grind.

The grind is going through the definitive agreement by section to gather, order, notify, build, and supply everything the agreement requires.

Legal counsel, hopefully, has put together a closing checklist for all to follow. If your legal counsel doesn't have it, ask them to ask the buyer's counsel if they have one, and get a copy. This process is another reason for hiring experienced bank M&A legal counsel so this can be as efficient as possible.

The closing checklist tracks everything needed to be done, who the responsible party is, and any notes or comments to keep everybody apprised of the status of each item along the way. If you would like a refresher on the items often included in the definitive agreement, please refer to Chapter 28 – Definitive Agreement & Disclosure Schedules.

One nice thing about the process at this point is that all employees are aware of the impending merger. That means you have more hands to assist in gathering details and data than you did prior to this.

Here is a general list of the items that may be included but not limited to on your closing checklist so you can get a flavor of the activities involved:

- Preparation of regulatory applications, for each regulatory agency (all applicable).

- Submission of regulatory applications, for each regulatory agency (all applicable).

- Notification of the merger requirements (possible newspaper publication).

- Estimated closing balance sheet tracking.

- Estimated closing shareholder's equity tracking.

- Engagement of the paying agent for cash merger consideration (if applicable).

- Engagement of the stock transfer agent for stock merger consideration (if applicable).

- Proxy materials provided to shareholders - this will be covered in detail in Chapter 35 - Shareholder Meeting.

- Notice of special shareholders meeting materials.

- Delivery of shareholder data to the paying agent for cash merger consideration (if applicable).

- Delivery of shareholder data to the stock transfer agent for stock merger consideration (if applicable).

- Termination of benefit plans.

- Shareholder approval election results.

- Directors and Officers (D&O) insurance tail coverage.

- Title(s) to real estate.

- Real estate survey(s).

- Environmental investigation(s).

- Termination of any deferred compensation plans & accrued payments.

- Termination of any company bonus programs or lump sum payments.

- Regulatory approvals from each regulatory agency (all applicable).

- Cash merger consideration to the paying agents (if applicable).

- Stock merger consideration to the stock transfer agent (if applicable).

- Board approval(s).

- Buyer's officer certificate.

- Seller's officer certificate.

- State(s) merger certificates (all applicable).

- Payment of accrued accounts under deferred compensation plan(s).

- Payment of bonus program lump sum(s).

- Third-party consents (provided to each vendor who has requirements for notice in their contract. If you had an annual board review of any material contracts, as suggested in Chapter 28 Definitive

Agreement & Disclosure Schedules, the requirement of having third-party consent could be tracked, making execution here much easier).

In addition to the closing checklist that legal counsel is following, as part of the access and investigation compliance and/or operation in the ordinary course of business activities agreed to in the definitive agreement, you will also have monthly (and periodic) reporting to the buyer of items that would generally include but are not be limited to:

- Monthly financial statements.

- Monthly budget comparisons.

- Monthly Asset/Liability Committee (ALCO) packets.

- Weekly loan committee agenda, approval packets and minutes.

- Monthly board packets.

Post-closing, there are items for tracking as well and generally the following would be included, but not limited to:

- Notification to regulators (all applicable).

- Return of the physical charter certificate to regulator.

- Circulation of the closing documents (full set).

- Form of the Letter of Transmittal from paying agent and/or stock transfer agent.

- Delivery of letter of transmittal(s) to shareholders.

- Payment of cash merger consideration (if applicable).

- Payment of stock merger consideration (if applicable).

- Release of conversion fund remainder (cash, if applicable, following an expiration of claim date).

- Change-In-Control payment(s) (if applicable).

- Stay-Put payment(s) (if applicable).

Nearly every item listed has an above-average level of work associated with it. There are items that will involve others outside of the buyer or seller's employment base, and you are subject to their calendars and cooperation. Those items that require the input of others, such as environmental inspections, title reports, real estate surveys, and D&O insurance tail coverage, should be engaged as soon as possible to allow for the time necessary to get them done. Third-party consents take time to send out and get back, regardless of how many you have. Again, if third-party consents are a part of your annual review of the vendor management program with the board, the information should be in good shape and ready for action. The process can feel like pushing a rope at times, but the pushing must continue until each item is complete.

There is no way to sugarcoat the process, and it is better mentally if you just embrace the grind.

The best way I can describe it is this:

The Daytona 500 is a 500-mile race on the 2.5-mile Daytona International Speedway track.

That's 200 laps.

This process is the 198 laps between the first lap (announcement) and the final lap (closing).

And they say in stock car racing, "Rubbing is racing."

There likely will be rubbing during the process, and patience wears thin on both sides.

Use your legal counsel and your investment bankers as your team when needed.

It will keep the buyer and seller relationship in the best possible shape at the end of the race.

You've got a special meeting of the shareholders coming up, let's look at that in the next chapter.

CHAPTER 35

SHAREHOLDER MEETING

L egal counsel should guide you through the process of calling a special meeting of the shareholders for the purpose of voting on the merger. Your corporate documents should spell this all out. Let your legal counsel review them and guide you to ensure things are done in accordance with those documents.

Side note: *If you are contemplating the sale of the bank at a point in the future, it would be a good process to familiarize yourself with the corporate documentation well in advance to understand the variables you will need to navigate should you decide to sell.*

The articles, bylaws, and shareholders agreement for both the bank and the holding company (if applicable) should be thoroughly reviewed. If there is anything that requires an update, you may wish to consider taking care of that as soon as possible, perhaps in alignment with an annual meeting. This also could be incorporated into your capital plan document as something that was reviewed in the event you need to raise capital, merge, or sell (for more information, please go to www.KurtKnutson.com/ BonusContent).

If your bylaws currently don't address the ability to deliver your proxy materials electronically, you may wish to revisit this with your legal counsel. During the COVID-19 global pandemic, many states updated their laws to include the electronic delivery of corporate documents and notices of meetings. Having the ability to provide notice for the meeting along with the proxy materials electronically allows for a less costly, trackable form of delivery that most shareholders prefer in today's post-pandemic environment.

It is even possible to send voting cards electronically as well. The voting card responses allow for a higher response rate and are very trackable and are date and time stamped. Being able to send electronic reminders of when proxy votes are due also helps increase the response rate.

All of this does require your shareholders to provide consent to receive the information electronically (follow the advice of your legal counsel), so the sooner you gain the ability to provide information in that manner, the better. That again may be in alignment with an annual meeting.

Generally, for the special meeting, the shareholders will be asked to vote in favor of the transaction. And if there are not enough votes on the first attempt to approve the merger, a second request the shareholders will be asked to approve is to allow for added time to gather the votes needed to meet the requirements for approval as supported in your corporate documents.

The proxy materials that are delivered to your shareholders (as guided by experienced legal counsel) generally include:

- Information related specifically to the special meeting, the voting rights and vote needed. How to vote and how to revoke proxies. The solicitation process for the proxies and the recommendation of the board of directors.

- Specific to the merger proposal, there would be a general description of what is being proposed to take place, what the merger consideration is, some background and reasons for the merger, the fairness opinion of the financial advisor (if the board sought one), the regulatory approval of the merger and any tax consequences of the merger. Additionally, appraisal rights, interests of the board of directors or management related to the transactions (including Change-In-Control and Stay-Put agreements, if applicable, and again the recommendation of the board of directors.

- Details of the definitive agreement such as the structure and effective date of the merger, the treatment of stock, the procedure for exchange of the stock, representations, and warranties, conduct of the business while the merger is pending, and the fact that no solicitation of acquisition proposals can take place. Also included are employee benefits information, and other covenants that may have been negotiated, conditions precedent to the merger, payment if there were to be a termination of the merger, expenses related to the merger, the effect of the merger on the rights of the shareholders and any voting agreements or restrictive covenants the board of directors and management must sign.

- The number of shares owned by the board of directors and executive officers.

- Copies of the various underlying documents in their entirety such as the definitive agreement, the fairness opinion, and the financial statements.

- And any other matters that may apply such as compliance with any state or federal legislation.

It may also be possible to hold the meeting electronically as well, if your corporate documents allow for that as well as any state and/or federal legislation requirements that may exist. I would advocate for the use of electronic communications if you possibly can throughout the process. Legal counsel can direct you in that regard. If the state and/or federal regulation allows for it, but your corporate documents do not, this is another item you may wish to update in conjunction with an annual meeting of the shareholders.

Following your special meeting, you will want to communicate to all shareholders the results of the meeting. If you can communicate electronically, an email immediately following the meeting sharing the results and next steps goes a long way towards shareholder satisfaction and answering questions. This approach saves shareholders time from having to ask for it themselves and saves your time and your team's time fielding and responding to those requests. The email is also trackable and can supply information related to opens and open rates that is helpful.

Regulatory approval will be running parallel to your preparation and the holding of your special meeting of the shareholders. You may or may not have regulatory approval prior to the meeting, and that should not hold up having the meeting. Shareholder approval can be subject to regulatory approval.

We'll talk about regulatory approval in the next chapter.

CHAPTER 36

REGULATORY APPROVAL

Regulatory approval is managed by the buyer.

If an application is "informationally complete," it is supposed to be approved 91 days after filing by statute. The process could be delayed by information requests from the regulators pushing the "informationally complete" clock. Fortunately, in our transaction, both banks were very clean, our market was adequately served, and the approval was within the time window. If both banks' combined assets are below $10 billion, and you are well-capitalized with strong asset quality, you likely will experience the same.

At the time of this writing, there have been conversations about updating the way bank mergers are assessed in terms of competition in serving communities and on financial stability. Again, this generally applies when one of the two parties' assets exceed $10 billion or that level is going to be exceeded with the combined banks. Regulators are operating from rules last updated in 1995, based on 1960s era standards.

Much has changed since 1995 in terms of access to financial products and services with the growth in online and mobile banking and the rise of non-bank competitors. M&A in rural communities have been especially impacted by the advanced growth of non-bank competition from credit unions, fintech's, credit card companies, and the U.S. Department of Agriculture's Farm Credit.

Farm Credit takes a rural bank's primary opportunity away from the community bank by way of real estate lending. When you think about a rural bank's biggest opportunity to make a loan, it is on real estate. That opportunity is primarily with a farmer or rancher and the real estate owned to support their livelihood. Financing real estate for a farmer or rancher is a substantial expense and any savings they can get on interest rates has a meaningful impact.

As a government agency and not subject to taxation, Farm Credit is able to loan money out at rates well below what a tax-paying bank can offer (but they typically do not offer the money at rates to the full extent of the tax benefit, usually just enough to win the deal).

In a step further, Farm Credit often wraps in the production loans by cross-collateralizing them with the real estate, further eroding the community bank's ability to offer production lending.

Consumer lending faces intense competition for rural banks as well. Mortgages from online mortgage lenders, auto loans from online lenders, auto dealers and manufacturers leave little behind to assure the survival of the community bank.

Farm Credit, online mortgage lenders, online consumer lenders and automobile manufacturers employ relatively few, and in most cases, no one in those rural communities.

Community banks need economies of scale to continue to exist. There is a certain level of fixed cost in running the bank. Accounting, human resources (HR), IT, loan operations, deposit operations and regulatory compliance functions are a big part of that. Regulatory and HR compliance are increasingly becoming more expensive.

When one bank buys another, the result is one set of each of these functions stays and the other goes away, along with the expense associated with it. Not all, but most. That's the scale I'm talking about. Increased regulation has a cost.

The old methods of competition calculation are no longer effective predictors of competition. Saying there aren't enough banks in a particular geographic area is no longer an accurate way to measure competition. The internet has changed that. Regulators have changed that. Non-bank providers have entered where banks have exited because it is too costly to provide some services. They too need modernization to consider the competition coming from government agencies, such as Farm Credit and other non-bank lenders.

Federal Reserve Board Governor Michelle "Miki" Bowman filled the long-vacated community bank seat at the Federal Reserve in 2018. It should be noted that the seat sat vacant during the financial crisis and the subsequent Dodd-Frank legislation. The seat sat vacant for 12 years prior to Governor Bowman's appointment. Community banks were missing that voice. Governor Bowman served as the Kansas banking commissioner and served as vice president of Farmers and Drovers Bank in Council Grove, Kansas, which her family helped establish.

Governor Bowman is aware that competition is at the foundation of our financial and economic system and is leading efforts to modernize the regulators' approach to competitive analysis. She as well as community bankers, their elected officials and trade associations need to make her voice heard and support her in her efforts.

I provide this context in the event the issue of competitive concerns arises. Nobody wants to publicly announce they have a deal only to have the deal die when seeking regulatory approval.

Once the buyer has received regulatory approval, you will want to share the news with your employees, customers, and shareholders. We'll be discussing the communication of the steps between announcing the signing of the definitive agreement and the closing in the next chapter.

CHAPTER 37

COMMUNICATION PLAN

When the announcement for the definitive agreement signing is made, you can only estimate when the closing will be because things like the regulatory approval timing are not in your control. So, your communication of the closing is typically within a range of a business quarter. Because of this, your comments on closing need to be very general, such as "We anticipate closing in the (first, second, third, or fourth) quarter."

Following the announcement, the buyer will be having team meetings on various topics surrounding the integration of the merger. It is very likely that your management will begin being a part of meetings that impact on their departments. You may or may not be involved in these meetings. This is the buyer's call. You have plenty to do, continuing to push towards closing. The process of gathering the information called for in the definitive agreement is called "confirmatory due diligence" as you are confirming the items the due diligence produced. Confirmatory due diligence, combined with the shareholder approval and preparing for the distribution of the merger consideration will require a great deal of your time.

In days past, when a bank merger was announced at closing, the signs changed, systems were converted and nearly everything was done over the period of a very long weekend. Today, there are usually three steps in the process that allow for the process to be a bit more deliberate.

Everybody would like a roadmap to help them get oriented to their surroundings, so communicating these steps to your employees following the announcement is important. This does need to be done with the buyer so there is no miscommunication, confusion, or chaos adding to the already large challenge of integrating the two banks.

The communication would likely flow as a three-step plan and could look something like this:

- **Step 1** – <u>From now until closing</u>:

    We continue to run the same way we always have.

    Our customers have the same products and services, they deal with the same people at the bank, our name doesn't change, and the logos are the same because the deal is not closed yet.

    We can't provide an exact date because we are awaiting regulatory approval along with shareholder approval, but we anticipate it will be in the next quarter.

    Once we have approvals and have a date planned, we will communicate the closing date with you, our employees, and our customers. We will also be communicating that closing date with the shareholders.

    As employees, you will be set up on the new payroll system, and you will be taken through an orientation on the new benefit plans you will be eligible to be a part of. The orientation will take place prior to closing, so that everything is effective on the first day as a (new bank) employee.

It was our practice through the years to hold all-employee meetings (we held two identical meetings, back-to-back so that half could attend while the other half tended to the business of the bank) the day after our board meeting each month. At those meetings, we would review the financial results for the month and year-to-date and compare the results to the budget. Following the financial presentation, we would then discuss an element of the culture.

We changed the cultural element of the meeting to supply any details we could about where we were on the journey to closing. I reminded the employees during these meetings that I was not speaking on behalf of the buyer and that I was only supplying information from our perspective and what I would anticipate the buyer to want to do.

As has been said many times throughout this book to this point, the deal was not closed, and until it was, you could not completely discount the chances that something could arise that would prevent us from closing.

Following that discussion, I tried to focus on career development topics to supply whatever help I could to ensure our employees of having continued success in the new organization or in their careers or life in general.

We were primarily a business bank, and we held weekly meetings covering our pipeline from opportunities through wins, losses, and closings along with product knowledge exercises. We continued these meetings as we did not want to stray from anything we had done to be successful. Employee participation remained consistent with our participation prior to the announcement. In addition, we embarked on a customer calling blitz so that we could meet in-person with as many people as possible. The goal was to reassure them that there was a great opportunity for them in terms of meeting their growth needs well into the future. We also reassured them that they would continue to be working with the people they were working with now. We continued our message discipline, staying on point with the announcement.

We continued with our advisory board meetings and invited representatives of the buyer to the meetings to see and to continue getting to know our advisory board members, whom they had personally met on the day of the announcement. These meetings were generally well-received by the Advisory Board. Attendance at these meetings remained consistent with our pre-announcement meetings as well.

So, from a communication standpoint, we were continually communicating with our shareholders, customers, and employees along the way and keeping the buyer informed of the touchpoints.

- **Step 2** – <u>From closing until conversion</u>:

    Once closing takes place—it typically will occur on a Friday—you (the employee) will leave the bank at the end of the day under our brand and return to the bank on Monday under the new brand.

    The website, the building, our emails, etc. will all be changed to reflect the new brand, *BUT other than brand*, nothing will change for the customer. Our customers will still login to online services and mobile banking as they have in the past and they will work with the same people they always have.

They don't need to change debit cards or checks; they all still work as they had prior to the closing.

We will communicate when and how things are changing, systems, products, etc., and will be communicating those changes to the customers throughout Step 2. We expect this period from closing to conversion to last six months (you will likely know when conversion will be at this point, as the buyer must reserve the date with the core provider).

During Step 2, you (the employee) will be interacting with your new counterparts, and that interaction will gain momentum as we make our way to the conversion date (Step 3). This will allow you to learn more about the new bank and its opportunities. It will also allow them to learn more about you, your goals, and your ambitions along the way.

You and our customers will begin to experience the opportunity that lies ahead of being part of a much larger organization with more opportunities, more locations, and more resources.

- **Step 3** – Conversion date:

  Once the conversion date occurs, all systems migrate from the seller to the buyer's bank. Debit cards will have been reissued with the new brand; new check stock ordered will carry the buyer's branding as well.

  There is only one website now, the buyer's. Online banking and treasury services logins are now on one system, the buyer's. Any trace of the legacy logos that couldn't be transitioned earlier, like online banking and treasury services because the transition was too costly to do twice (one changing the logo to the buyer's logo on the seller's system, and then the second time when the seller's system converts to the buyer's system), are now gone.

Continued calling efforts to this point have really made this last change a non-event for customers and employees. There will be some rough spots that will need to be corrected where the conversion of the information didn't make it over to the correct location in the database. Those will get corrected as they are discovered.

And again, all employees will have time during Step 2 to become familiar with the new bank and will have time to make the transition by the time we get to Step 3.

As you can see, our primary responsibility for crafting communication was to get the customers and employees to and through closing. The buyer was responsible for crafting the message from closing forward.

We still needed to craft the communication to our shareholders post-closing, as ours was an all-cash transaction, and they needed to be shepherded through to receipt of their merger consideration.

And while we were not crafting the communication message for our customers and employees going forward, we were still very much responsible for communicating, which we will cover in the next chapter.

Side Note: *From the meeting with our board, the first broaching the topic of selling to closing on the merger was 320 days or 10 ½ months. That is about as fast as this process can go. This information is being provided for perspective and planning purposes.*

SECTION 5

POST-CLOSING

CHAPTER 38

COMMUNICATE, COMMUNICATE, COMMUNICATE

You've closed on the merger. Legal counsel has communicated that everything is done. Documents have been exchanged and the deal has closed.

The paying agent has the funds for distributing the cash merger consideration when shares are surrendered, according to the instructions the shareholders will receive in their letter of transmittal.

It is important to remind you that your bank's internal accounts go away at closing—they now belong to the buyer—an important consideration and reminder for getting expense reimbursements submitted prior to closing. As such, payments were wired earlier in the day to both legal counsel and the investment bankers.

It's time to communicate this milestone with everybody.

Employees, customers, and shareholders.

Everybody is finally on board.

By now, the employees have been exposed to so much activity since the announcement, this news is met with relief that communication will begin in earnest and directly with their new employer. A strange mixture of melancholy and excitement clings to those involved.

The employees have been given instructions about the new payroll system to use beginning Monday.

Customers have also been hearing about the combination for about 90 days and, to a great degree, are looking to what the future holds. If Step 1 (see Chapter 36 – Communication Plan) has been executed properly, they are comfortable with the fact that other than branding, their business has not been disrupted in much of any way and the closing is a non-event.

Shareholders are made aware of the closing and know they will be receiving instructions as to how they collect their merger consideration.

The website has been updated to announce the merger has been closed. The branding has changed on the site to the new logo. The colors of the website have changed to match the buyer's brand palette. Online banking login reflects that it is the legacy online banking link. The press release and frequently asked questions (FAQs) from the announcement remain on the site and now joining those documents is a welcome message from the buyer's CEO. The legacy website can either be used, or the legacy domain could point to the buyer's website, depending on the buyer's preference.

I would recommend to the buyers out there reading this that if the legacy bank domain is not going to be used, at least forward the domain to the new site. If the domain is taken down, either at closing or later, it appears to the customer that the bank is no longer in business. Similarly, Apple maps or Google maps need to be transitioned to the new name from the existing listings as opposed to stopping the existing listing and creating new ones. Customers (or prospects), who may not be familiar with the transaction or remember the buyer's name yet could get a business closed message when searching using the legacy name.

Social media sites have been updated to spread the word the merger has closed and encourage followers to follow the new brand's social media sites. The legacy social media sites will remain through conversion, with no further posts being made beyond the posts pointing to the buyer's social media sites.

Stay disciplined and on message. The announcement talking points should be as relevant today as they were during the announcement.

What about the old brand?

What happens with all the items carrying the legacy brand?

It may not be as clear cut as you think.

We'll cover that in the next chapter.

CHAPTER 39

BRANDING

All your employees left Friday under your brand.

They will be arriving on Monday as employees of the new brand.

There is a great deal of work that needs to be done by the seller over the weekend to prepare for that change.

The sign company needs to be ready to change out signs over the weekend at all your locations. That could mean full sign change outs or banners being placed over your existing signs. New letterhead, envelopes, product materials, interior signage, etc., all need to be brought in and organized.

There are buyers who prefer to wipe the old brand and start new. Everything goes to the dumpster.

Other buyers gather all the materials, letterhead, envelopes, corporate apparel, logoed items, branded pictures, etc., and are respectful of the old brand while incorporating the new. They understand the emotional attachment the seller's employees have had in building the brand.

It varies by buyer.

As a buyer, you have paid for the right to do as you please. However, you may want to consider the latter rather than the former.

Again, you have made a large investment in the purchase of the bank. You have hopes and dreams of the talent staying on and being fantastic contributors to your organization going forward. You want the talent to communicate to the customers their excitement for the new bank, so your odds rise of retaining those customers through the change.

Why risk starting off on the wrong foot on day one?

Gather the legacy branded items in one location and give the employees an opportunity to help themselves to it. Just ask that they take the former logoed items home in return. Think of a goodwill message that could let them know they have done a wonderful job of building a valued brand and that you want that to be a part of their legacy. Then let them know you want them to carry that same desire to build the brand to the new brand. In fact, you're counting on it!

It's a small gesture but it makes a huge statement to the employees.

You're honoring their past contributions and showing respect as they are welcomed in. It's asking them for their support.

Business is hard.

As the buyer, you need all the easy wins you can get.

It's an easy win if done well. If done incorrectly, the buyer will overdraw their goodwill account with employees right from the start and will have to work very hard to get the "balance" back in positive territory.

There are similar considerations that may apply to the Change-In-Control (CIC) payments and Stay-Puts, if you have them, as well. We'll cover that in the next chapter.

CHAPTER 40

CHANGE-IN-CONTROL PAYMENTS AND STAY-PUT AGREEMENTS

As a practical matter, Change-In-Control agreements generally call for the lump sum payment due within 30 days of the change-in-control event. Buyers may wish to consider making the lump sum payment at the time of the closing. Everybody should be happy with the terms outlined in the agreement, but as a practical matter, the buyer has already agreed to pay them, and it is a very strong signal of goodwill if it is paid at closing.

There is a great opportunity to start things off with a strong indication of goodwill if a check were to be delivered to the homes of the individuals who earned it with a personal welcome message from the buyer. It sends a completely different message than showing up as a direct deposit two weeks later. It sets the tone for a strong relationship going forward.

A buyer may be hesitant to make such an effort because they are uncertain about the employee's role going forward in the combined organization and may not want to be that bold because they feel it could change leverage in the relationship going forward. This is a "playing not to lose" mindset, and you've just made a huge investment on a win.

The same train of thought may come into play regarding Stay-Put payments as well. The buyer has already made the decision to honor the Stay-Put agreements when they were the successful bidder. A more proactive mindset with the new talent can be a great opportunity to shape the combined organization. The buyer has all the leverage with the new talent. Be more proactive in your approach with your new talent. The Stay-Put payment will be made if the employee delivers on their end and stays past the required Stay-Put period, typically 12 months. If the buyer decides the employee is not what they were looking for, they can opt to terminate the employee, make the Stay-Put payment with a physical check (preferably delivered, by hand or via overnight delivery, on the date of earning it or termination. Even the termination can be done in a positive tone when (and if) the time comes.

It's a great opportunity for a buyer, in my opinion, to be proactive and to utilize their talent for their advantage right out of the gate. Change is always a great time to adjust across the entire organization.

The merger may be closed, but you, as the seller, have still got to get the cash (and or stock) merger proceeds in the hands of your shareholders. From their perspective, they sold their house, the buyers have moved in, and they haven't received their money (or stock). How does this work?

We'll cover that in the next chapter.

Chapter 41

CONVERSION OF SHARES

The deal has closed, the signs have changed, and as you can imagine, the shareholders are interested in when they receive the merger consideration. When they sell a home, the documents get signed and the keys are exchanged for the sales proceeds.

This transaction isn't that simple, so communication is the key to having things go as smoothly as possible.

The details are a bit different depending on whether you were selling for cash, selling for stock, or selling for a cash and stock combination. What is the same for all three scenarios, however, is that they will need to send their stock certificate in.

So, the first thing they need to do is to make sure they can find their physical certificate(s). That can be communicated as early as the day of the announcement and repeated with all correspondence following that.

In the event a stock certificate(s) cannot be found, you will want to collaborate with legal counsel to get that remedied. Paying agents and stock transfer agents will charge a fair amount to remedy it, and it will more than likely take time. So, these issues need to be corrected as early as possible. You will also need to provide the paying agent and/or the stock transfer agent with shareholder data in the form in which their systems process the data. The buyer's legal counsel will work through your legal counsel to get you the instructions for properly submitting the data.

You will need social security numbers (EINs in the case of IRA custodians or corporate shareholders), addresses, proper titling, number of shares, phone numbers, and email addresses all to be current and ready to go. So, if you have work to do there, get started on that as soon as possible, going back as far as the announcement day so it isn't something you're working on while people are awaiting their merger proceeds.

There will be an instruction letter sent to the shareholders called a "Letter of Transmittal." The letter of transmittal provides the instructions to the shareholders for surrendering their stock certificates. It is important for you to get a copy of the letter of transmittal as soon as you can. That may not be until the last 30 days or so prior to closing. You want to get a copy so that you can understand the message that is going out to your shareholders. That way, you're informed on the matter and can answer any questions shareholders present to you.

The letters of transmittal going out to shareholders will likely be sent via the U.S. Postal Service (USPS). For that reason, you will want to ask to be provided with electronic copies of letters that have gone out. You will want those copies for three reasons:

1) To make sure the certificates went to the right people with the correct information.

2) So that you can ensure the address is correct when a shareholder calls and says they haven't received theirs yet.

3) So that you can use that letter as a substitute in the event they don't receive their letter.

Because the letters went out via the United States Postal Service (USPS), the delivery times of those letters will be all over the board. You should be prepared for this.

Depending on the number of shareholders you have, this process could take a fair amount of time for everybody to get their merger proceeds. Communication is the key to a smooth outcome here. When in doubt, keep them informed. Even if there is little new information to report, say "There is little new information to report since our last communication." It takes the worry away from your shareholders that a communication has been missed.

In the case of cash proceeds, there likely will be a point in time, typically a year from closing, where cash not collected will revert to the buyer. Not being able to locate a shareholder and shareholder apathy with one or two will likely be the reason for failure to collect, as crazy as it sounds.

Stay on top of collections so that this doesn't come into play. Exhaust all efforts to find and communicate with the shareholders. It's easy to think you have more than enough time to get this done, but time will go by faster than you realize. Similarly, continue to push shareholders to collect their proceeds for the same reason.

Even though you have been mindful of communicating with customers from announcement to closing, they have moved to the top of your competitors' calling lists. You will want to get back out in front of them following closing. We'll cover that in the next chapter.

CHAPTER 42

CUSTOMER MEETING BLITZ

In addition to the organic customer calling that has taken place since the announcement, you had a customer calling blitz as well. That is a concentrated effort to go to the customer's place of business for a face-to-face meeting or perhaps taking them to lunch. The goal of the calling blitz was to make certain you are able to alleviate any fears they might have in regard to their own business being disrupted.

It may seem like you just did this. You did within the past 90 days, but following the closing of the merger it will need to be done again.

Never be concerned with over communicating.

Your competition has been calling on your customers non-stop since the announcement. They are likely going to be ramping it up further post-closing.

It is important also to understand that switching to a competitor comes at a cost. It is very disruptive to your customer's business. What they *really* want is to not have their bank become a distraction to what they do on a day-to-day basis.

They want to know that the calling officer they have invested time and effort into understanding their business will be the same. They want to know they are not going to be going through abrupt product or pricing changes without an ability to smoothly incorporate the changes into their business. And they want to know the "new guys," know who they are, respect them, and want to do business with them. If you aren't making the overtures on a frequent basis, the customer will fill in the blanks in their mind about how they will be treated in the future. They will be more open to taking calls from the competition and may not move right away, but each of those calls from the competition could potentially weaken the relationship.

The customers are less interested in logo items and statements about who you are. Those statements that may be true but are boring and have no meaning because they are said by everybody all the time. "We want to be your trusted advisor." It's pointless static if those words are not accompanied by actions.

There is a natural tendency to turn inward and focus on the changes going on in your own world post-closing, but that urge needs to be tempered with the need to call on customers.

If the new senior credit officer can accompany you on calls, it is even better. Having your customers know they are meeting an important decision maker with the new bank is important.

The top 10 or even the top 20 customers may warrant taking the new CEO with you. Prep the new CEO in advance of the meeting even if they don't ask for it. Instruct relationship managers to put together a briefing document that identifies the key players in the business, how long the business has been around, a brief financial snapshot, what is important to them, why they bank with you, what they may be interested in hearing about from the new CEO, the extent of the relationship with the bank and deliver it to the CEO at least 24 hours in advance of the meeting. The relationship manager needs to understand if they do this, they will become the go-to person for the CEO. Help them out. Their value will rise, and the customer will feel appreciated.

It's the right thing to do.

Instruct the relationship managers to do the same for the senior credit officer too. Even though the senior credit officer is very aware who the customer is from the due diligence process, make it easy for them. The relationship manager will be seen at a higher level in their eyes as well because you prepare, and your value will continue to rise.

The same can be said for meeting with the employees. We'll cover that in the next chapter.

CHAPTER 43

EMPLOYEE MEETING BLITZ

This chapter is primarily for the buyers reading the book. It is going to seem an awful lot like the last chapter you just read, except the word "customer" is being replaced by the word "employee."

This is being provided as an aid to make your acquisition go as successfully as possible. Please read it in the spirit in which it is intended. If you get good at this, you will distinguish yourself in your employees' eyes and that, in turn, will be felt by your customers.

In addition to the employee interaction that has taken place since the announcement, you had an employee meeting blitz as well. By that I mean a concentrated effort to sit down for a face-to-face meeting with each employee. The goal of the employee meeting blitz was to make certain you can alleviate any fears they have that their role in the bank is being disrupted by the change.

It may seem like you just did this within the past 90 days, but it's time to do it again following the closing of the merger.

There's no such thing as over communicating.

Your competition has been calling on your newly attained employees non-stop since the announcement. They are likely going to be ramping it up further post-closing.

It is important also to understand that switching to another employer comes at a cost. It is very disruptive to your employee's life. What they really want is to not have their employer become a distraction to what they do on a day-to-day basis.

They want to know that the time they have invested in their career is going to be put to good use. They want to know they are not going to be going through abrupt role or wage and benefit changes without an ability to smoothly incorporate the changes into their lives. And they want to know the "new guys" know who they are, respect them, and want them.

The employees are less interested in logo items branded with the new brand and statements about who you are. Those statements that may be true but are boring and have no meaning because they are said by everybody all the time. "We care about our employees." It's just a static sound if not accompanied by actions proving the claim.

I guess the only good thing about corporate platitudes is that you can count on the competition's message to your employees is, "We're *reaching out* to see if you're *interested in an exploratory call* to see if there are *potential synergies.*" Terms and phrases that mean nothing but sound cool. It's filler. That kind of talk takes the place of the real work they need to do to communicate the role they are recruiting for.

There is a natural tendency to turn inward to focus on the changes going on in your world post-closing, but that urge needs to be tempered with the need to call on the new employees.

It's the right thing to do.

You have made a major investment and are counting on the future earnings power of the bank you just acquired to pay for the acquisition and contribute to even higher earnings for the combined bank.

The work you put into the year following the closing date, if done properly, will pay repeatedly into the future.

Resist the temptation to think, "Well, that's done. What's next?"

You have too much riding on this.

This chapter is a reminder to all CEOs of the selling bank. Things are no longer your call. We'll cover that in the next chapter.

CHAPTER 44

NO LONGER YOUR CALL

W ith the closing, the bank you were CEO of, and the holding company (if applicable) no longer exists. The duties you had related to the distribution of the merger consideration do remain until they have been fully disbursed.

But as mentioned in Chapter 36 – Communication Plan, once the merger was announced, employees and customers begin to look beyond your authority to the new "final word." That means your duties as the official "final word" went away when the merger closed.

This isn't a surprise and it's not meant to be depressing or to highlight the obvious. The main point in covering it is that with the proper perspective, it can be liberating. The inescapable issues related to customers, employees, and shareholders now don't solely rest on your shoulders.

If a decision is made that maybe is a long way away from a decision you would have made, so be it. The buyer paid a lot of money to have the right to make that decision, and all you can do is provide input and carry out that decision. In fact, being a good advocate is all that you can do now.

I've witnessed both business owners who've sold their business and employees who have been acquired wrestle with this. I have wrestled with it previously, as selling the bank we built wasn't the first time I was a part of a bank that was acquired. In fact, it's what eventually led to starting my own bank.

Hopefully the situation will be great for all parties involved, but if it isn't or if you're no longer needed, just move on. No need to try to belabor the point, no need to try to influence others or make them live through your struggles, just move on.

I was fully aware of the fact that I was going to ultimately be the most duplicated person involved when and if we ever sold. The value in the organization was in the development of the team, the systems and processes that didn't require my involvement on a day-to-day basis. My role was to be looking out over the next three to five years to provide direction and that would no longer be needed because the buyer has that role taken care of.

I will enjoy watching the bank continue to grow, hearing about the development of our employees' careers, and seeing the continued growth of our customers and their impact on the community. Our customers bring more job opportunities to the community, their employees purchase homes, they increase trade in the community which in turn provides the resources for better schools and services. And hopefully our shareholders can redeploy the capital that was returned to them for even more growth in our community.

Will I miss the opportunity to continue to guide the bank into the future? You bet.

But I am glad I was able to be a part of it and want all involved to be successful.

The bank provided opportunities that would not have been presented had I not gone down this path. I'm sure you feel the same way. I have worked with people that most people would only dream of being able to call co-workers; they are very talented and caring people. I have been able to participate in our industry associations and for the state with great people as well. The bank and a career in banking has been good to me and my family.

I thank everybody involved along the way and wish them all continued success.

Along with things no longer resting squarely on your shoulders, your responsibilities will change as well. It is important to understand those changes because they can add a spring to your step. We'll cover this in more detail in the next chapter.

CHAPTER 45

RESPONSIBILITY CHANGES

The buyer will be providing direction for your responsibilities post-closing. Most notably it will be to make the transition as smooth as possible, keep the customers happy, assist the team through the transition, bring in new business, collaborate with the new team members, and be a positive addition to the culture.

There are responsibilities you'll no longer have post-closing as well.

It is worth mentioning because one has a way of thinking of change as adding to your already long list of things you need to accomplish. That's not actually the case here. Change can bring rejuvenation to your career with the right perspective. You'll be able to reclaim some of your time, which will be a trade-off for the new responsibilities.

Think through the responsibilities you have that are periodic such as exams. You will still participate in them, but you now aren't ultimately accountable for the results and the follow-up.

Think about the annual duties you have that you, again, likely will participate in but are ultimately not accountable for the entire project. Things like the annual business plan and the budget. The annual shareholders meeting and all that goes with it from preparing the proxy materials to delivering them and to preparing for and holding the meeting.

Think about the quarterly duties such as call report preparation, review, and submission. And the preparation and review of the quarterly board reports like the interest rate sensitivity analysis, ACH and remote deposit capture review, and the review of the allowance for loan and lease losses report.

No more monthly board meetings to prepare for. Or monthly Asset/Liability Committee (ALCO) meetings to assemble information, review and prepare for. No more monthly all-employee meetings to prepare for the review of financials in comparison to budget and to cover elements of the culture.

These activities, while extremely important, all took a lot of your time.

We haven't even touched on the weekly and daily responsibilities. Think about all of those as well.

You may have enjoyed a great many of them and will feel a loss about not being involved in them directly any longer. Some you will be glad to see it go.

You should also think about the recovery time you will have.

Charge your batteries a bit before moving forward.

Vacation? What's that?

A change in your perspective will likely do wonders for you but you likely have had no time to even consider these things until now.

Celebration—we're going to cover that in the next chapter.

CHAPTER 46

CELEBRATION DINNERS

MANAGEMENT TEAM

It's important to celebrate this milestone with your team and to affirm their transformation into the value-driven leaders they have become.

Sadly, many leaders are so competitive when we finally accomplish a goal, we don't 'waste time' on celebrating because we are already moving onto the next challenge. I have been guilty of that myself.

What you need to keep in mind is most people are not so obsessively self-motivated. They would like to be acknowledged. Specifically, they want to hear from their leader that a win was truly a win.

A win worthy of celebrating.

It's important they hear, "You've changed. You're different now. You're stronger, more competent, more capable. Congratulations. You did it."

Celebrating the win is how you let them know they've changed, they've become more competent, stronger, and more capable.

The celebration needs to be memorialized and it should be relative to the success. A dinner at a very nice restaurant with your team and their spouses or special guests would be worthy of consideration and would demonstrate your appreciation.

As the leader, you should memorialize it with words as well. The team can't read your mind. Letting everybody know why you are celebrating is important. You need to let them know how much they've changed since the day they became a part of the team.

You don't need to go through each individual and the individual changes that have taken place in this group setting. But you do need to ask them to think back on who they were on the day they first walked in. Then point out the accomplishments the team has made ultimately ending in the win. Ask them to think about who they are now, and all the things they can do now versus the day they walked in.

A transformation has taken place for every one of them.

They have changed. They are different. They are stronger, more competent, and more capable.

Nobody can ever take that away from them.

This dinner with the team may be best to have six to nine months following closing. Allow the changes to settle in. By the time you have this dinner, some may no longer be with the buyer but an invitation is extended because the dinner is a celebration for the people who built the bank to what it was prior to the change-in-control, others may now be past the head-spinning changes and at a place where the message can be heard.

The point of this dinner isn't to focus on the present—it is to celebrate them and their transformation with this win.

INVESTMENT BANKERS/DEAL TEAM

Another celebration dinner you will likely have will be with the investment bankers as their guests. The attendees for this dinner can take many different shapes and forms from the board, the board and spouses and guests, to the deal team, or the deal team and spouses or guests, to the management team and management team and spouses or guests. The choice is often left up to the seller.

The investment bankers gave us the option to choose who we wanted to attend our closing dinner. We chose to have this dinner be the deal team only. The deal team and the investment bankers form a bond during this time because they are working closely with one another.

We chose to have the dinner about 60 days after closing, so the conversation was naturally going to involve many of the stories about the transaction and we thought it best to stick with the deal team. It was a wonderful evening and appreciated greatly by our team.

Your experience could be something totally different. Your investment bankers may choose to have a closing dinner or may not. They may have their own idea of who should attend or may leave it up to you.

BOARD

An additional celebration dinner we had was just the board. No spouses or guests or deal team or management. Just the board.

These were the people remaining, the ones who were there from the start.

It was important to me to have a celebration dinner with them where we could speak freely about the bank through the entire process from the start of the bank through the sale and not bore spouses with boring "work talk."

This dinner was about 90 days after closing. The timing was chosen because it was far enough along to let the transaction closing settle out. To allow for all to decompress and have some time to reflect.

I am providing what we did and the thought processes involved just so you have examples in which to add to your individual planning process. How you manage this is entirely your call.

It is very important though to celebrate the win, to memorialize the transformation with words, and thank those responsible.

Well, there it is. You've gone through the bank sale process from idea to celebration. Not from an accounting perspective, or legal perspective or the perspective of an investment banker, but from the perspective of a CEO.

ABOUT THE AUTHOR

Kurt Knutson was a banker for four decades. In 2005, he organized and led a group of local businesspeople to form Freedom Bank, headquartered in Overland Park, Kansas. Freedom Bank opened its doors in 2006 and provided over a half of a billion dollars in capital to privately held companies throughout the Kansas City area. Freedom Bank sold in October of 2022 delivering a return to the shareholders that outperformed the S&P 500 for the same investment period.

Kurt was appointed by the Governor to the Kansas State Banking Board where he served as Chairman. He was elected by his peers as Chairman of the Kansas Bankers Association and was a member of the American Bankers Association Government Relations Council.

Kurt and the team at Freedom Bank started a non-profit called the Freedom Founders Forward Foundation as a dynamic platform for informing, educating, and connecting Freedom Bank's community and constituents with a wide spectrum of philanthropic opportunities. The causes ranged from teen suicide prevention to veteran's assistance with mobility, meals, and support dogs to equipping inmates to function as positive and productive members of society both inside prison and upon release.

The foundation also had an emphasis on financial literacy and established the Corporate Finance Academy, a nine-week paid internship at Freedom Bank that was designed to provide insights to business students with the complementary skills of common sense, people sense, and street smarts in an active and positive real-world environment.

Kurt and Freedom Bank also played an active role in the Blue Valley School District's Center for Advanced Professional Studies ("CAPS") profession-based learning, which was founded as a single school district program in 2009 and is now the model for 100 affiliate locations spanning 170 school districts in 23 states and four countries. The original Global Business Class for CAPS was housed in Freedom Bank and the students actively participated in the business.

Today, Kurt is Chairman of his growing business Knutson Enterprises, LLC which operates two business brands—Strategic Options and Level 3 Freedom.

Learn more at www.KurtKnutson.com.

URGENT PLEA!

Thank You for Reading My Book!
I really appreciate all your feedback and
I love hearing what you have to say.

I need your input to make the next version of
this book and my future books better.

Please take two minutes now to leave a helpful review
on Amazon letting me know what you thought of the
book:

Go to: www.KurtKnutson.com/Review

Thank you so much!
Kurt Knutson

Made in the USA
Columbia, SC
23 January 2025